# Building Chatbots with Python

Using Natural Language Processing and Machine Learning

Sumit Raj

APress®

*Building Chatbots with Python*

Sumit Raj
Bangalore, Karnataka, India

ISBN-13 (pbk): 978-1-4842-4095-3          ISBN-13 (electronic): 978-1-4842-4096-0
https://doi.org/10.1007/978-1-4842-4096-0

Library of Congress Control Number: 2018965181

Managing Director, Apress Media LLC: Welmoed Spahr
Acquisitions Editor: Nikhil Karkal
Development Editor: Matthew Moodie
Coordinating Editor: Divya Modi

Cover designed by eStudioCalamar

Cover image designed by Freepik (www.freepik.com)

Distributed to the book trade worldwide by Springer Science+Business Media New York, 233 Spring Street, 6th Floor, New York, NY 10013. Phone 1-800-SPRINGER, fax (201) 348-4505, e-mail orders-ny@springer-sbm.com, or visit www.springeronline.com. Apress Media, LLC is a California LLC and the sole member (owner) is Springer Science + Business Media Finance Inc (SSBM Finance Inc). SSBM Finance Inc is a **Delaware** corporation.

For information on translations, please e-mail rights@apress.com, or visit http://www.apress.com/rights-permissions.

Apress titles may be purchased in bulk for academic, corporate, or promotional use. eBook versions and licenses are also available for most titles. For more information, reference our Print and eBook Bulk Sales web page at http://www.apress.com/bulk-sales.

Any source code or other supplementary material referenced by the author in this book is available to readers on GitHub via the book's product page, located at www.apress.com/978-1-4842-4095-3. For more detailed information, please visit http://www.apress.com/source-code.

Printed on acid-free paper

*I want to dedicate this book and all the hard work to achieve this feat to my elder brother, Nikhil Raj, whom I lost this year. I can't seem to imagine how proud he would have been seeing his brother's book being published today.*

*I would like to thank my parents Dinanath Prasad and Shobha Gupta, my brother and sister, relatives, and all my dearest friends who always supported & encouraged me and pardoned my absence at times during the write-up of this book.*

# Table of Contents

# About the Author

**Sumit Raj** is a techie at heart, who loves coding and building applications. He is a Python expert with a keen interest in Machine Learning and Natural Language Processing. He believes in the idea of writing code that directly impacts the revenue of the company.

Sumit has worked in multiple domains, such as personal finance management, real estate, e-commerce, and revenue analytics, to build multiple scalable applications. He has helped various early age startups with their initial design and architecture of the product, which was later funded by investors and governments. He comes with a good experience of cutting-edge technologies used in high-volume internet/enterprise applications for scalability, performance tuning, and optimization and cost-reduction.

He has been mentoring students/developers on Python programming all across the globe. He has mentored over 1000 students and professionals using various online and offline platforms and channels on programming languages, data science, and for career counseling. Sumit likes to be a part of technical meetups, conferences, and workshops. He never likes to miss a chance to attend hackathons. His love for building applications and problem solving has won him multiple awards and accolades. He is regularly invited to speak at premier educational institutes of India. He is also a speaker at PyLadies meetup group, ladies who code in Python, which is led by one of the former director of PSF (Python Software Foundation).

In his free time, he likes to write on his blog and answer questions on computer programming, chatbots, Python/Django, career advice, and web development on Quora, having over 1 million views together. Feel free to A2A on his Quora profile.

Currently, Sumit is working as Senior Solutions Architect at GeoSpark R&D in Bangalore, India, building a developer platform for location tracking. You can get to know more about him from his website (`https://sumitraj.in`). Readers can also ask their questions and discuss at, `https://buildingchatbotswithpython.sumitraj.in/`.

# About the Technical Reviewer

**Nitin Solanki** has extensive experience in Natural Language Processing, Machine Learning, and Artificial Intelligence Chatbot development. He has developed AI chatbots in various domains, such as healthcare, e-commerce, education and law firms, and more. He has experience working on NLP libraries, data mining, data cleansing, feature engineering, data analytics and visualization, and machine learning algorithms. Nitin loves to make things simple and automated. In his spare time, his mind starts chattering about ideas to make money. Therefore, he keeps his mind busy in exploring technologies and in writing codes.

# Acknowledgments

This book is an outcome of most sincere hard work that I have done in my career. Lots of sleepless nights have gone into the completion of this book. I will be grateful to my father and mother for my entire life because they made me who am I am today. I want to thank my brother Nitish and sister Prity for always being there and sharing the high level of understanding and emotions without being told.

This acknowledgment can't be completed without thanking the awesome Apress Team, including Nikhil and Divya, who have been so patient and supportive of me from the acquisition through the publication of the book. They are the best people to work with. Special thanks to Matt for all the guidance I needed for my first book and continued feedback at every step to improve the book. Huge thanks to Nitin for technically reviewing the book and suggesting the edits.

# Introduction

This book has been written with immense care to keep the teachings from this book very pragmatic and results-oriented. Building chatbots is not just about completing a tutorial or following a few steps—it's a skill in itself. This book will certainly not bore you with lots of text and process to be read; rather, it takes the learning-by-doing approach. You must have used at least one chatbot to do something in your life by now. Whether you are a programmer or not, once you go through this book you will find the building blocks of chatbots, and all the mysteries will be uncovered. Building chatbots may seem difficult from the outside, but this book makes it so easy for you. Our brain is not designed to directly process the complex concepts; rather, we learn step-by-step. When you are reading this book, from the first chapter through the last chapter, you will find how clearly things are progressing. Although you can directly go to any chapter, I highly recommend you start from the first chapter, as it is bound to bolster your thoughts.

This book is like a web series where you won't be able to resist the next chapter after completing one. Any chatbot that you interact with after going through this book will create a picture in your mind on how that chatbot is designed and built internally.

## Who This Book Is For

This book will serve as a great resource for learning the concepts related to chatbots and learning how to build them. Those who will find this book useful include:

- Python web developers looking to expand their knowledge or career into chatbots development

- Students and aspiring programmers wanting to acquire a new skill set by hands-on experience to showcase something and stand out in the crowd

- Natural Language enthusiasts looking to learn how to build a chatbot from scratch

- Budding entrepreneurs with a great idea but not enough technical feasibility information on how to go about making a chatbot

- Product/Engineering managers planning for a chatbot-related project

# How Do I Approach This Book?

Remember this book is not written like other books are written. This book is written keeping in mind that once you are done with this book, you can build a chatbot yourself or teach someone how to build a chatbot. It's very important to keep a few points in mind before approaching this book like any other book:

- This book covers almost everything that you need to build a chatbot, rather than what exists.

- This book is about spending more time in doing things on your system, with this book by your side. Make sure you execute each code snippet and try to write the code; do not copy and paste.

- Make sure you follow the steps as they appear in the book; don't worry if you don't understand something. You will get to know about that later in the chapter.

- Use the source code and Jupyter Notebook provided with this book for your reference.

# What Will You Learn in This Book?

**Chapter 1: The Beloved Chatbots** In this chapter you will get to know about things related to chatbots from both a business and developer's perspective. This chapter sets the tone for getting our hands dirty with chatbots concepts and converting them into code. Hopefully, you will have a reason why you should definitely build a chatbot for yourself or your company by the end of this chapter.

**Chapter 2: Natural Language Processing for Chatbots** In this chapter you will learn about what tools and methods to use when NLP is needed for chatbots. This chapter not only teaches you about the method in NLP but also takes real-life examples and demonstrates with coding examples. This chapter also discusses why a particular NLP method may be needed in chatbots. Note that NLP in itself is a skill to have.

**Chapter 3: Building Chatbots the Easy Way** In this chapter you will learn about building a chatbot in a nice and easy manner using tools like Dialogflow. If you are a non-programmer, you will surely like it, as it requires little or no programming skills.

**Chapter 4: Building Chatbots the Hard Way** In this chapter, you will learn about building chatbots in a manner that people want to build. The title says the hard way, but once you have completed the previous chapter, you will be wanting more, as this chapter will teach how to build chatbots in-house from scratch and how to train chatbots using machine learning algorithms.

**Chapter 5: Deploying Your Chatbot** This chapter is purely designed to give your chatbot app a final push. When you have come through the easy and hard way of building a chatbot, you will surely not want to keep it to yourself. You will learn how to showcase your chatbots to the world using Facebook and Slack and, finally, integrate them on your own website.

# CHAPTER 1

# The Beloved Chatbots

When you begin to build a chatbot, it's very important to understand what chatbots do and what they look like.

You must have heard of Siri, IBM Watson, Google Allo, etc. The basic problem that these bots try to solve is to become an intermediary and help users become more productive. They do this by allowing the user to worry less about how information will be retrieved and about the input format that may be needed to attain specific data. Bots tend to become more and more intelligent as they handle user data input and gain more insights from it. Chatbots are successful because they give you exactly what you want.

Does it irritate you or frustrate you when you have to enter the same name, e-mail ID, address, and pincode every time on different websites? Imagine a single bot that does your tasks—say, ordering food from different vendors, shopping online from various e-commerce companies, or booking a flight or train tickets—and you don't have to provide the same e-mail ID, shipping address, or payment information every time. The bot has the capability to know this information already and is intelligent enough to retrieve what is needed when you ask it in your own language or in what is known in computer science as Natural Language.

Chatbots development is way easier than it was a few years ago, but chatbots did exist decades ago as well; however, the popularity of chatbots has increased exponentially in last few years.

If you are a technical person or have some idea of how a web application or mobile application works, then you must have heard the term APIs. Any kind of data that you need today is available to be consumed in the form of APIs provided by different service providers and institutions. If you are looking for weather information, booking tickets, ordering food, getting flight information, converting one language to another, or posting on Facebook or Twitter, all of this can be done using APIs. These APIs are used by web- or mobile-based applications to do these tasks. Chatbots can also use these APIs to achieve the same tasks based on our requests.

1

© Sumit Raj 2019
S. Raj, *Building Chatbots with Python*, https://doi.org/10.1007/978-1-4842-4096-0_1

The reason Chatbots get an edge over traditional methods of getting things done online is you can do multiple things with the help of a chatbot. It's not just a chatbot, it's like your virtual personal assistant. You can think of being able to book a hotel room on booking.com as well as booking a table in a nearby restaurant of the hotel, but you can do that using your chatbot. Chatbots fulfill the need of being multipurpose and hence save a lot of time and money.

In this book we are going to learn how to build natural conversational experiences using bots and how to teach a bot to understand our natural language and make it do tasks for us from a single interface.

Bots in general are nothing but a machine that is intelligent enough to understand your request and then formulate your request in such a way that is understandable by other software systems to request the data you need.

# Popularity of Chatbots Usage

Chatbots have become popular just as anything from the recent past. Let's try looking at Figure 1-1, which depicts the rise of chatbots, and also try to understand why there is a huge demand for building chatbots.

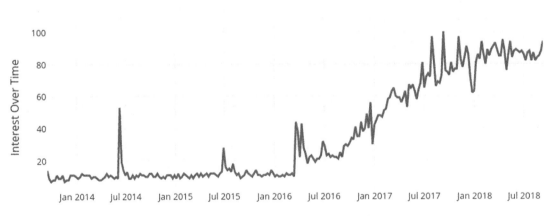

*Figure 1-1.* *Numbers on Y-axis represent search interest relative to the highest point on the chart across all categories worldwide*

The simple answer that comes to mind is that it's not a complex software and can be used by anyone. When we build software we target the audience who will be using it, but when it's used by anyone else, it becomes difficult and unusable. When we build chatbots we keep in mind that it will be used by people of all age groups. This happens only in case of chatbots, where the software tries to behave like a dumb person (but it's intelligent) and lets the user be who he or she is. In all other software, you will find that you should be aware of some terminologies or gradually be aware of how to optimally make use of it, but that's not the case with chatbots. If you know how to talk to a person, you won't have any issue using a chatbot.

There is a continuous growing demand for chatbots. However, there has not been much research that has empirically tried finding out the motivations behind using chatbots. In a recent study, an online questionnaire asked chatbot users ages 16 to 55 years from the US to describe their need for using chatbots in their daily lives. The survey revealed the "productivity" to be the primary motivational factor for using chatbots.

## The Zen of Python and Why It Applies to Chatbots?

I remember the Zen of Python, which says, "Simple is better than Complex," and that applies so many places in software.

> *The Zen of Python is a collection of 20 software principles that influences the design of Python Programming Language.*
>
> —Tim Peters

Want to know *"What is Zen of Python?"* Try the below steps.

If you already have Python installed on your computer. Just go to your Python interpreter and import this:

```
Python 2.7.15 (default, May  1 2018, 16:44:08)
[GCC 4.2.1 Compatible Apple LLVM 9.1.0 (clang-902.0.39.1)] on darwin
Type "help", "copyright", "credits" or "license" for more information.
>>> import this
The Zen of Python, by Tim Peters

Beautiful is better than ugly.
Explicit is better than implicit.
```

Simple is better than complex.
Complex is better than complicated.
Flat is better than nested.
Sparse is better than dense.
Readability counts.
Special cases aren't special enough to break the rules.
Although practicality beats `purity.
Errors should never pass silently.
Unless explicitly silenced.
In the face of ambiguity, refuse the temptation to guess.
There should be one—and preferably only one—obvious way to do it.
Although that way may not be obvious at first unless you're Dutch.
Now is better than never.
Although never is often better than *right* now.
If the implementation is hard to explain, it's a bad idea.
If the implementation is easy to explain, it may be a good idea.
Namespaces are one honking great idea—let's do more of those!

You may not able to make sense of all points above relating to chatbots but surely you can most of them.

Well, coming back to our topic, I remember finding difficulty starting to use Facebook User Interface while coming from Orkut background. If you have never used Orkut, you would not understand it, but just try thinking of a situation in your life where you started using some new software or application and you had a hard time getting the hang of it. Maybe switching from Windows to MacOS/Linux or vice versa? When you use a new application, you need to learn a few things, and it takes time to get used to it and to know what it does and how it works. It does happen at times that you come to know some features of the application even after years of using it. If you are on MacOS, try Shift + Option + Volume Up/Down and see what happens. Let me know if it amazed you, if you didn't know it already.

In the case of chatbots, the communication between the user and the server or backend system is pretty simple. It's just like talking to some other person using a messaging app.

You just type what you want, and the bot should be able to either give you what you want or should guide you how to get that. In other words, it should point you to the correct information by giving you a link or document. The time has come where bots are able to even dig up the information from an article and document and provide it to the users.

Significant progress in AI by companies like Google, Facebook, and IBM and by machine learning services like Amazon Lex, wit.ai, api.ai, luis.ai, IBM Watson, Amazon Echo, etc. has led to the extraordinary growth and demand of such robots.

# The Need for Chatbots

Now, we will try to look at the need and demand of chatbots in this fast-growing information creation and retrieval age from two different perspectives: the business standpoint and the developer's perspective. So, if you are a product manager, sales manager, or from marketing or any related domain that drives the business directly, then you should not skip the business perspective of the chatbots. It will give you a clear picture that businesses today need to adopt this technology to drive more revenue.

# The Business Perspective

We will try to look at the business perspective of the chatbots. Is it good for a business to have a chatbot or to migrate lots of stuff to be done by chatbots?

The time has already come for businesses to treat chatbots as one of the marketing tools of this generation.

- **Accessibility:** They are easily accessible. The consumer can open the website and start asking questions or begin resolving their queries without having to dial a number and follow the ugly way of "Press 1 for this and Press 2 for that" in the IVR. They can quickly get to the point with just a basic set of information.

- **Efficiency:** Customers can sit at their desk in their office or on a couch in their living room while watching a game and get their status of a credit card application, find their food order status, or raise a complaint about any issue.

If you make customers efficient and productive, they start loving you. Bots do exactly that and help boost business.

- **Availability:** Chatbots are available 24 hours per day, 7 days per week. They would never ask you for leaves or get tired like human employees. They will do the same tasks or new tasks every time with the same efficiency and performance. You must get frustrated when some customer care phone number says, "Please call us between 9:00 AM and 6:00 PM," just for a piece of information. Your bots would never say this.

- **Scalability:** One Bot => 1 million employees. You see this? Yes, if your bot can do what a customer needs, it can easily handle hundreds of thousands of customer queries at the same time without breaking a sweat. You don't need to keep your customers waiting in queue until the customer representative becomes free.

- **Cost:** Needless to say it saves a hell of a lot of cost for the business. Who doesn't like to save money? When bots do that for you, there is no reason why you shouldn't like them.

- **Insights:** Your sales representative might not be able to remember the behavior of the user and give you exclusive insight about the consumer behavioral pattern, but your bots can using latest techniques of machine learning and data science.

## Chatbots Bring Revenue

Chatbots have proven to be successful in bringing more revenue to the business. Businesses starting with chatbot support or creating a new chatbot to support customer queries are doing well in the market compared to their competitors.

As per one of the blogposts on stanfy.com, in the first 2 months after introducing its Facebook chatbot, 1-800-Flowers.com reported that more than 70 percent of its Messenger orders were from new customers. These new customers were also generally younger than the company's typical shopper, as they were already familiar with the Facebook Messenger app. This significantly increased their annual revenue.

*One of the greatest added values of chatbots is using them for generating prospects. You can reach your potential clients directly where their attention is (messengers) and present them your newest products, services or goods. When a customer would like to purchase a product/service, he/she can make the purchase within the chatbot, including the payment process. Bots, like 1-800flowers.com, eBay, and Fynd have already proved that.*

—Julien Blancher, Co-Founder @ Recast.AI

In an article by Stefan Kojouharov, founder of ChatbotsLife, he mentions how different companies are making more money than they would have without chatbots. He says,

The e-commerce space has begun using chatbots in a number of ways that are quickly adding dollars to their bottom line. Let's look at the early success stories:

- **1–800-Flowers:** reported that more than 70 percent of its Messenger orders derived from new customers!

- **Sephora:** increased their makeover appointments by 11 percent via their Facebook Messenger chatbot.

- **Nitro Café:** increased sales by 20 percent with their Messenger chatbot, which was designed for easy ordering, direct payments, and instant two-way communication.

- **Sun's Soccer:** chatbots drove nearly 50 percent of its users back to their site throughout specific soccer coverage; 43 percent of chatbot subscribers clicked through during their best period.

- **Asos:** increased orders by 300 percent using Messenger chatbots and got a 250 percent return on Spend while reaching 3.5 times more people.

  Figure 1-2 tries to give you an idea of why there is a direct correlation between chatbots and revenue. Lets have a look at Figure 1-2 to get some idea about that.

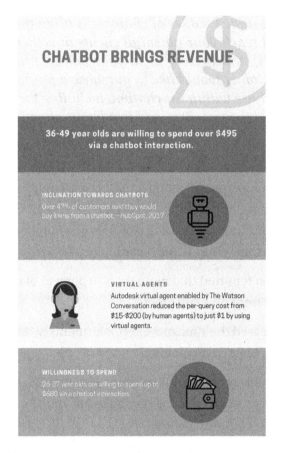

**Figure 1-2.**  *Chatbot brings revenue*

## A Glimpse of Chatbot Usage

We will try to look at how useful chatbot has been for consumers due to its usability and the efficiency it provides. Everybody in this burning IT age wants to be fast in everything, and using chatbots makes your jobs easier and faster every day. It is personalized in a way as to not repeat obvious things; this makes us re-think about traditional usage of software. Figure 1-3 provides an illustration that should give you a fair idea about chatbot usage.

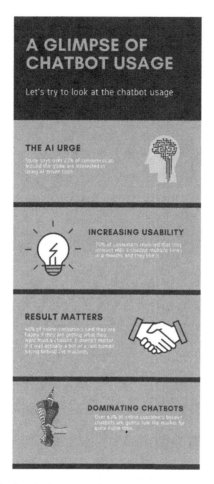

*Figure 1-3.* *A glimpse of Chatbot usage by consumers*

## Customers Prefer Chatbots

Chatbots are not just software in the modern era. Chatbots are like our personal assistants who understand us and can be microconfigured. They remember our likes and dislikes and never tend to disappoint us by forgetting what we taught them already, and this is the reason why everyone loves chatbot. Next time you meet a person or meet your customer, don't forget to ask if they prefer conventional software or the new cutting-edge chatbots. Lets have a look at Figure 1-4 to understand the reasons why customers prefer chatbots compared to other software systems for human computer interactions.

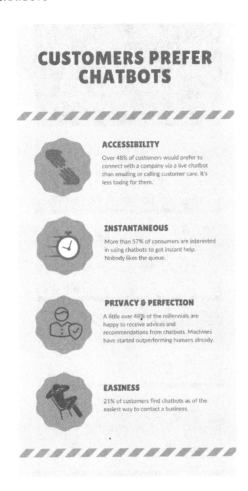

***Figure 1-4.*** *Customers prefer chatbots*

In the next section of this chapter we are going to discuss why chatbots are the next big thing for budding developers. Whether you are a newer or a mid-level developer or an experienced SME you must understand what is available to developers when building chatbots.

# The Developer's Perspective

Have you ever felt the pain when you have to update the OS of your computer or phone or any other app that you might be using in order to use new features? What if there is not much need to update the app every time to use new features? Or say, instead of having multiple apps, one could have one single app that did most of the things currently done by multiple apps?

Bots for developers are fun to build. It's like teaching your kid to walk, talk, behave, and do things. You love making it more intelligent and self-sufficient. From a developer's perspective, chatbots are a very important subject to know about.

## Feature Releases and Bug Fixes

Lots of features can be added to the chatbot painlessly without having your users update your chatbot app. It might be a pain in the neck if you released a version of the app with some bug, and you have to fix it and release again in the AppStore for approval, and, most importantly, the users will have to update the app after all. If they don't update, then the customer will keep complaining about the issue, which results in productivity loss for everyone. In chatbots, everything is API-based, so you just fix the issue in the backend, deploy the changes in PRODUCTION, and woaah—issue fixed for your users without any worry. You save lots of time from user-reported bugs as well.

Imagine you built a bot to find restaurants and later you wanted to add the capability of searching for hotels, flights, etc. Users can easily just request such information, and your backend chatbot system will take care of everything.

Suppose you are building a Facebook Messenger chatbot; you can control almost everything, including what interface the user sees in his app, directly from your backend. In Facebook Messenger bots, you can choose whether the user gets to click on a button to say Yes/No or just enters simple text.

## Market Demand

Fifty-four percent of the developers worldwide worked on chatbots for the first time in 2016. There is a huge demand for building a simple chatbot that works for companies, and they are looking for developers who can build it for them. Once you have completed Chapter 3 of this book I bet you can start selling your services to companies easily. You can also do your own startup in an area of your expertise by introducing a chatbot for that domain. Being able to build a chatbot end-to-end is a new skill to have, and that's the reason average market pay is also very good for chatbot developers.

The growing demand for chatbots can be seen in the number of chatbots being developed on developer platforms like Facebook. Facebook has 100,000 monthly active bots on the Messenger platform, and counting. You will be amazed to know that Messenger had 600 million users in April 2015, growing to 900 million in June 2016, 1 billion in July 2016, and 1.2 billion in April 2017.

## Learning Curve

Whether you are from a frontend/backend background or know very little programming, there is immense possibility to learn new things when you are building or learning to build a chatbot. In this process you will learn about many things. For example, you get to learn more about Human Computer Interaction (HCI), which talks about the design and use of computer technology, focused on the interfaces between people and computers. You will be learning how to build or use APIs or web services, using third-party APIs like Google APIs, Twitter APIs, Uber APIs, etc. You will have immense opportunity to learn about Natural Language Processing, machine learning, consumer behavior, and many other technical and non-technical things.

# Industries Impacted by Chatbots

Let's have a quick look at the industries that will benefit most from chatbots. A research study by Mindbowser in association with *Chatbots Journal* collected data from 300+ individuals who participated from a wide array of industries including online retail, aviation, logistics, supply chain, e-commerce, hospitality, education, technology, manufacturing, and marketing & advertising. If we look at the chart in Figure 1-5, it is pretty much evident that e-commerce, insurance, healthcare, and retail are the industries benefiting most from chatbots. These industries rely heavily upon the responsiveness of the customer care team in an efficient manner that saves time. Given the fact that chatbot is good at that, it is evident that it will hail in these industries pretty quickly.

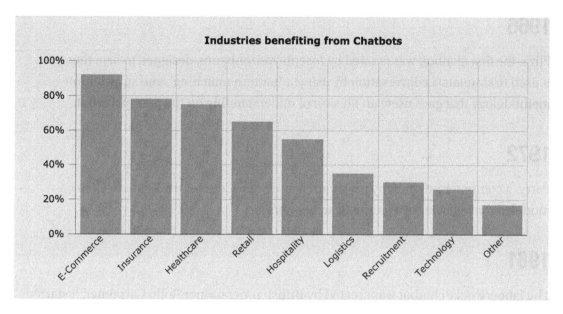

**Figure 1-5.** *Top industries that will benefit most from chatbots*

At this point of time, the chatbots are still getting traction in newer sectors in different forms. The next 5 to 10 years will be very much crucial for chatbots to spread the word in different industries that have no experience working with chatbots.

# Brief Timeline of Chatbots

Let's look at the brief history of the timeline of how chatbots were formulated. It's very important to know where chatbot technology came from and how it was shaped. Chatbots have certainly gained popularity recently but the efforts are being made using decades of work with this technology. The history of chatbots will certainly amaze you regarding how far we have come since we started.

# 1950

The Turing test was developed by Alan Turing. It was a test of a machine's ability to exhibit intelligent behavior equivalent to, or indistinguishable from, that of a human.

# 1966

Eliza, the first chatbot, was created by Joseph Weizenbaum, designed to be a therapist. It used to simulate a conversation by using a "pattern matching" and substitution methodology that gave users an illusion of understanding on the part of the bot.

# 1972

Parry, a computer program by psychiatrist and Stanford scientist Kenneth Colby, modeled the behavior of a paranoid schizophrenic.

# 1981

The Jabberwocky chatbot was created by British programmer Rollo Carpenter. It started in 1981 and launched on internet in 1997.

The aim of this chatbot was to "simulate natural human chat in an interesting, entertaining and humorous manner."

# 1985

The wireless robot toy, Tomy Chatbot, repeats any message recorded on its tape.

# 1992

Dr. Sbaitso, a chatbot created by Creative Labs for MS-DOS, "conversed" with the user as if it were a psychologist in a digitized voice. Repeated swearing and malformed input from the users caused Dr. Sbaitso to "break down" in a "PARITY ERROR" before it could reset itself.

# 1995

A.L.I.C.E (Artificial Linguistic Internet Computer Entity) was developed by Nobel Prize winner Richard Wallace.

# 1996

Hex, developed by Jason Hutchens, was based on Eliza and won the Loebner Prize in 1996.

# 2001

Smarterchild, an intelligent bot developed by ActiveBuddy, was widely distributed across global instance messaging and SMS networks. The original implementation quickly grew to provide instant access to news, weather, stock information, movie times, yellow pages listings, and detailed sports data, as well as a variety of tools (personal assistant, calculators, translator, etc.).

# 2006

The idea of Watson was coined from a dinner table; it was being designed to compete on the TV show "Jeopardy." In its first pass it could only get about 15 percent of answers correct, but later Watson was able to beat human contestants on a regular basis.

# 2010

Siri, an intelligent personal assistant, was launched as an iPhone app and then integrated as a part of the iOS. Siri is a spin-out from the SRI International Artificial Intelligence Center. Its speech recognition engine was provided by Nuance Communications, and Siri uses advanced machine learning technologies to function.

# 2012

Google launched the Google Now chatbot. It was originally codenamed "Majel" after Majel Barrett, the wife of Gene Roddenberry and the voice of computer systems in the Star Trek franchise; it was also codenamed as "assistant."

# 2014

Amazon released Alexa. The word "Alexa" has a hard consonant with the X, and therefore it can be recognized with higher precision. This was the primary reason Amazon chose this name.

## 2015

Cortana, a virtual assistant created by Microsoft. Cortana can set reminders, recognize natural voice, and answer questions using information from the Bing search engine. It was named after a fictional artificial intelligence character in the Halo video game series.

## 2016

In April 2016, Facebook announced a bot platform for Messenger, including APIs to build chatbots to interact with users. Later enhancements done included bots being able to participate in groups, preview screens, and QR scan capability through Messenger's camera functionality to take users directly to the bot.

In May 2016, Google unveiled its Amazon Echo competitor voice-enabled bot called Google Home at the company's developer conference. It enables users to speak voice commands to interact with various services.

## 2017

Woebot is an automated conversational agent that helps you monitor mood, learn about yourself, and makes you feel better. Woebot uses a combination of NLP techniques, psychological expertise (**Cognitive-behavioral therapy** [CBT]), excellent writing, and a sense of humor to treat depression.

# What Kind of Problems Can I Solve Using Chatbots?

This question becomes challenging when you don't know the scope of your bot or don't want to limit it to answer queries.

It's very important to remember that there is a limit to what chatbots can do. It always feels that we are talking to a human-like thing that is very intelligent, but the specific bot is designed and trained to behave in a certain way and solve a specific problem only. It cannot do everything, at least as of now. The future is definitely bright.

So, we come to the question of finding out if your problem statement is really good to go and you can build a bot around it.

If the answer to all of these three questions is yes, then you are good to go.

# Can the Problem be Solved by Simple Question and Answer or Back-and-Forth Communication?

It's really important to not try to be a hero when solving any problem that is very new to you. You should always aim to keep the problem scope limited. Build the basic functionality and then add on top of it. Don't try to make it complex in the first cut itself. It doesn't work in software.

Imagine Mark Zuckerberg thinking out loud and spending time building all the features of Facebook at the start. Tagging a friend, having a like button, liking a user comment, better messaging, live video, reactions on comments, etc.—these features didn't exist even when Facebook was funded with over 1 million registered users on the platform. Would he have really succeeded if he would have gone on to first build these features and then launch the platform?

So, we should always try to create features only needed at the moment without having to over-engineer things.

Now, coming back to the first question, "Can the problem be solved by simple question and answer or back-and-forth communication?"

You just have to keep your scope limited and your answer will be yes. We are not at all limiting ourselves to solving complex problems but definitely limiting ourselves to solving a complex problem all in one go.

*"You have to make every single detail perfect. And you have to limit the number of details."*

—Jack Dorsey

# Does It Have Highly Repetitive Issues That Require Either Analyzing or Fetching of Data?

This question is important because either from a business perspective or a developer's perspective, what chatbot does and is made to do is to make people using it efficient and productive. And how do you do that? By removing the need of a user to do repetitive things themselves.

Chatbots are definitely more capable of just automating some highly repetitive stuff, but you will always find that most of the chatbots primarily try to solve the same issue—be it by learning under supervision (read: "By Supervised Learning") or self-teaching (read: "By Un-supervised Learning").

## Can Your Bot's Task be Automated and Fixed?

Unless you are thinking of building a chatbot just for your learning purpose, you should make sure the problem you are trying to solve can be automated. Machines have started to learn and do things themselves, but still it's a very nascent stage. What you think can't be automated now may be automated in a few years.

## A QnA Bot

One of the good examples of a problem statement for building a chatbot could be a QnA Bot. Imagine a bot that is trained to understand various user questions whose answers are already available on an FAQ page of a website.

If you go back and try to find the answer of the aforementioned three questions, the answer will be yes.

See Figure 1-6 and you will find what an FAQ bot is doing.

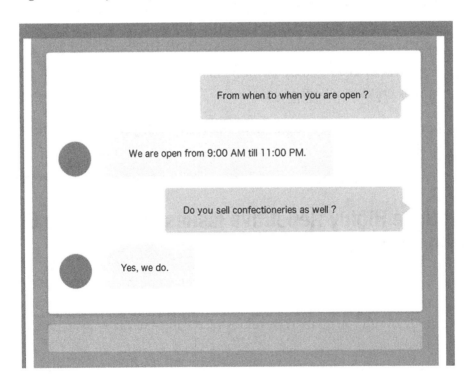

*Figure 1-6.* *FAQ chatbot example*

These are nothing but very repetitive questions that customers of a particular store may call and ask or try to find answers to by going to a website and navigating through the pages.

Think when you have a chatbot like this and it answers your question like a human in seconds and even does more than you could imagine. This is just a little of what chatbots are capable of.

Now, let's try to analyze the aforementioned three questions and their answers in case of QnA Bot.

- Can the problem be solved by simple question and answer or back-and-forth communication?

  Yes, FAQs are nothing but simple frequently asked questions and their relative answers. There may be a context-based FAQ, but unless you are solving a multidomain problem using chatbots, you won't be having this problem. There could be a situation where two or more questions may seem similar, but you can always design the bot to ask a question back to the user when it's doubtful.

- Does it have highly repetitive issues that require either analyzing or fetching of data?

  Yes, FAQs require us to fetch the data from the database and show it all at once in the website or possibly dynamically. But the user has to go through all questions one by one to find the question he/she is looking for and then see its answer. Lots of combing through the UI before the consumer actually gets his/her answer... or maybe not. Why not let our bot do that for us?

- Can your bot's task be automated and fixed?

  Yes, an FAQ bot would need to get the question, analyze the question, fetch information from the database, and give it back to the user. There is nothing here that can't be done using coding. And also, the process it pretty much fixed won't change in real-time.

# Starting With Chatbots

There are three steps one should follow before building chatbots. We'll discuss each one of them briefly here.

1.  Think about all the scenarios or tasks you want your chatbot to be able to do, and gather all related questions in different forms that can be asked to do those tasks. Every task that you want your chatbot to do will define an **intent**.

2.  Each question that you list or intent can be represented in multiple ways. It depends on how the user expresses it.

    For example: Alexa, Switch off the light. Alexa, Would you please switch off the light? Can you please switch off the light? A user may use any of these sentences to instruct the bot to switch off the light. All of these have the same intent/task to switch off the light, but they are being asked in different **utterances**/**variances**.

3.  Write all your logic to keep the user tied to the flow that you have chosen after you recognize the user's intent.

    For example, suppose you are building a bot to book a doctor's appointment. Then you ask your user to give a phone number, name, and specialist, and then you show the slots and then book it.

In this case you can expect the user to know these details and not try to accommodate all the things in the bot itself, like a specialist for an ear problem is called an ENT. However, doing this is not a big deal. So, again it comes back to deciding the scope of your bot, depending on the time and resource you have to build the application.

# Decision Trees in Chatbots

If you know about <u>decision trees</u>, then that's very good because you will be needing that knowledge frequently when designing the flow of your chatbots. But if you don't know about the decision trees, then just Googling would help you learn this simple concept widely used in Computer Science.

# Using Decision Trees in Chatbots

In the context of chatbots, a decision tree simply assists us in finding the exact answer to a user's question.

*A decision tree is a decision support tool that uses a tree-like graph or model of decisions and their possible consequences, including chance event outcomes, resource costs, and utility. It is one way to display an algorithm that only contains conditional control statements.*

—Wikipedia

The most difficult part when building a chatbot is to keep track of if...else code blocks. The greater the number of decisions to make, the more frequently if...else comes up in the code. But at the same time these blocks are required to encode the complex conversational flows. If the problem is complex and requires a lot of if...else in real-life, then that will require code to adjust in the same way.

# How Does a Decision Tree Help?

Decision trees are simple to write and understand, but they are a powerful representation of the solution made for the problem in question. They inherit a unique capability to help us understand a lot of things.

- Help in creating a full picture of the problem at hand. Looking at the decision tree, we can easily understand what's missing or what needs to be modified.

- Helps debug faster. Decision trees are like a short bible or, say, a visual representation of a software requirement specification document, which can be referred by developers, product managers, or leadership to explain the expected behavior or make any changes if needed.

- AI is still not at that stage that it can be trained with lots of data and perform with 100 percent accuracy. It still requires a lot of hand-holding by writing business logic and rules. Decision trees help wherever it becomes a little tough to ask a machine to learn and do it.

Let's take a simple example and try to understand how it helps in building chatbots. Look at the example diagram for a chatbot that starts with a question of whether the user is looking for a t-shirt or jeans, and based on the input the diagram flow goes further to give options related to the product by asking more questions. You don't need to create a full-fledged decision tree, but you should definitely have a flow of questions defined at every step before starting to build chatbots.

Suppose you were building a similar chatbot that helps people buy apparel online. The first thing you would do is to make a similar decision tree or a flowchart to help your chatbot ask appropriate questions at the right time. This is really needed to set the scope of each step and what needs to be done at that stage. You will need the state diagrams or a simple flowchart later when you actually code your first chatbot. Remember to not be too stringent while creating a diagram like Figure 1-7; keep it as simple as possible and then add the extended functionalities later. The benefit of such a process is the development time will be cut down, and later on the functionality will be loosely coupled and would start making sense as components. Like in the example, after creating the basic functionality, you can add color choices, price range, ratings, and discount options as well.

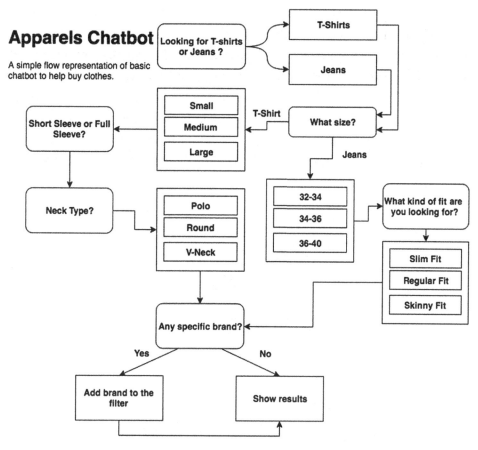

***Figure 1-7.*** *A simple representation of an apparel chatbot for buying clothes online*

There are definitely more things you can add to the earlier use-case depending upon your requirements. But you have to make sure that you don't make it too complex for yourself as well as for the user.

A decision tree not only helps you to keep the user tied to the flow but also is a very effective way to identify the next intent that might be coming in the form of a question from the customer.

So, your bot will ask a series of questions following the decision tree that you have built. Each node narrows down on the customer's goal through chatbot intents.

Suppose you were creating a chatbot for a financial institution—say, a bank—that can do a money transfer based on your request after authentication. In this case, your bot may first want to verify the account details and ask the user to confirm the amount, and then the bot may ask to validate target account name, account number, account type, etc.

You cannot or would not want to invoke an OTP (one-time password) API unless you have validated if the user's account balance is more than the requested amount.

It happens with all of us and with customers as well. They get frustrated when their questions are not answered correctly. Using decision trees for your chatbot will definitely make the experience better for your users than it would be if your didn't use them.

Lots of times you will find issues solving some intents programmatically. So, the bottom line is, *"If you can't solve something programmatically then solve it by design."*

Look at Figure 1-8 where the bot is trying to take a health quiz and wants to know if antibiotics can work for everything.

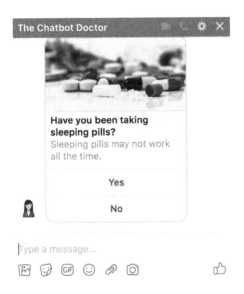

***Figure 1-8.** Example of solving a use-case by design*

Since the answer is expected to be a Boolean (True/False), you give just two buttons for the user to click instead of letting them type and wait to fix their mistake.

This is solving by design rather than writing lots of code that will be handling unexpected user inputs. You will have so many scenarios while building the chatbots where by just giving buttons, you will be able to quickly know the intent of the user. It's important to understand such scenarios and provide buttons both for your own convenience as well as for users who don't need to type in obvious cases of optional answers.

# The Best Chatbots/Bot Frameworks

- https://woebot.io/
    - Can track your mood
    - Helps you feel better
    - Gives you insights by seeing your mood pattern
    - Teaches you how to be positive and high-energy
- https://qnamaker.ai/
    - Build, train, and publish a simple question-and-answer bot based on FAQ, URLs, and structured documents in minutes.
    - Test and refine responses using a familiar chat interface.
- https://dialogflow.com/
    - Formerly known as api.ai and widely popular among chatbot enthusiasts.
    - Give users new ways to interact with your product by building engaging voice-and text-based conversational interfaces powered by AI.
    - Connect with users on the Google Assistant, Amazon Alexa, Facebook Messenger, and other popular platforms and devices.
    - Analyzes and understands the user's intent to help you respond in the most useful way.
- https://core.rasa.ai
    - A framework for building conversational software
    - You can implement the actions your bot can take in Python code.
    - Rather than a bunch of if...else statements, the logic of your bot is based on a probabilistic model trained on example conversations.

- https://wit.ai

  - Wit.ai makes it easy for developers to build applications and devices that you can talk or text to.

  - Acquired by Facebook within 21 months of its launch, wit.ai team contributes toward Facebook's own NLP engine inside Facebook.

  - You can use wit.ai for building chatbots, home automation, etc.

  - Wit.ai is similar to the way Dialogflow works but is not as feature-rich as Dialogflow. People initially used wit.ai, as it was free and Dialogflow was not, but later on Dialogflow became free as well.

- https://www.luis.ai/

  - A machine learning-based service to build natural language into apps, bots, and IoT devices.

  - Quickly create enterprise-ready, custom models that continuously improve.

- http://botkit.ai

  - Visual conversation builder

  - Built-in stats and metrics

  - Can be easily integrated with Facebook, Microsoft, IBM Watson, Slack, Telegram, etc.

# Components of a Chatbot and Terminologies Used

Components of a chatbot system are very few. In this section we'll be briefly discussing the components of a chatbot that you will come across in the later chapters.

Having a basic theoretical understanding of any system before diving deep is always helpful. You should have a fair idea after this section about technical terminologies used while building chatbots using Python. These terminologies will be used frequently in coming chapters when we actually start building our chatbots.

# Intent

When a user interacts with a chatbot, what is his intention to use the chatbot/what is he asking for?

For example, when a user says, "Book a movie ticket," to a chatbot, we as humans can understand that the user wants to book a movie ticket. This is intent for a bot. It could be named "*book_movie*" intent.

Another example could be when a user says, "I want to order food," or "Can you help me order food?" These could be named "*order_food*" intent. Likewise, you can define as many intents as you want.

# Entities

Intents have metadata about the intent called "**Entities.**" In the example, "Book a movie ticket," booking a ticket could be an intent and the entity is "**movie,**" which could have been something else as well, like flight, concert, etc.

You can have general entities labeled for use throughout the intents. Entities could represent as a quantity, count, or volume. Intents can have multiple entities as well.

For example: Order me a shoe of size 8.

There could be two entities here:

Category: Shoe

Size: 8

# Utterances

Utterances are nothing but different forms of the same question/intent your user may show.

- Remember we discussed the switching off the light intent? That was an example of how a user can use different utterances for the same intent.

- It is suggested to have an optimum 10 utterances per intent and a minimum of 5, but this is not restricted.

# Training the Bot

Training essentially means to build a model that will learn from the existing set of defined intents/entities and utterances on how to categorize the new utterances and provide a confidence score along with it.

When we train the system using utterances, this is called supervised learning. We will soon be learning more about doing this practically.

# Confidence Score

Every time you try to find what intent an utterance may belong to, your model will come up with a confidence score. This score tells you how confident your machine learning model is about recognizing the intent of the user.

That's all we wanted to cover in the first chapter of "Introduction to Chatbots." You must have a fair idea about chatbots from a business perspective and from a technical perspective. We walked through the lane of history belonging to chatbots. It's quite fascinating how far chatbots have evolved.

We learned about how chatbots have evolved over a period of time and why chatbots are a must for a business to grow in this cutthroat competition. We learned about the different chatbot frameworks and also got to know about the terminology used for chatbots by example. We'll be using them in the coming chapters. You should be at a stage now where you know what kind of chatbot you want to build and how it would behave when built.

Do all your write-ups and decision trees, if needed, and after we have learned the basics of Natural Language Understanding in the next chapter, we can quickly start building our chatbot.

Don't worry even if you don't have anything in mind. We'll try to build a cool chatbot step by step with all the concepts learned in the upcoming chapters.

See you in the next chapter.

# CHAPTER 2

# Natural Language Processing for Chatbots

This chapter is to get you started with Natural Language Processing (NLP) using Python needed to build chatbots. You will learn the basic methods and techniques of NLP using an awesome open-source library called spaCy. If you are a beginner or intermediate to the Python ecosystem, then do not worry, as you'll get to do every step that is needed to learn NLP for chatbots. This chapter not only teaches you about the methods in NLP but also takes real-life examples and demonstrates them with coding examples. We'll also discuss why a particular NLP method may be needed for chatbots. Note that NLP in itself is a skill.

We'll be closely taking a look at POS tagging, stemming, entity detection, stopwords, dependency parsing, and noun chunks and finding similarity between words. All of these methods will be very helpful for you when you are building chatbots of your use-case.

There are a lot more NLP methods than the ones covered in this chapter. Based on your need for the chatbot you are building, you can try to learn them. The SpaCy library that we are going to learn to use by the end of this chapter will give you enough idea on how to scale your knowledge base of NLP and its understanding. So, let's get started and first try to understand NLP for chatbots in the next section.

## Why Do I Need to Know Natural Language Processing to Build a Chatbot?

To understand the answer to this question, let's first understand Natural Language Processing (NLP).

**Natural Language Processing (NLP)** is a field of Artificial Intelligence that enables computers to analyze and understand the human language.

29

© Sumit Raj 2019
S. Raj, *Building Chatbots with Python*, https://doi.org/10.1007/978-1-4842-4096-0_2

Now, to perform NLP or, say, Natural Language Understanding (NLU), we have lots of methods that we are going to discuss next. You heard a new term **Natural Language Understanding (NLU)**—what is that now?

In simple terms, NLU is a subset of a bigger picture of NLP, just like machine learning, deep learning, NLP, and data mining are a subset of a bigger picture of Artificial Intelligence(AI), which is an umbrella term for any computer program that does something smart.

> *A good rule of thumb is to use the term NLU to express a machine's ability to understand the natural language in a form provided by humans.*

Now, coming to the question of whether you really need to know NLP to build a chatbot—the answer is both Yes and No. Confused? You heard it right, it's not that you can't build a chatbot at all if you don't know the method and techniques of NLP, but your scope will be somewhat limited. You won't be able to scale the application and keep the code clean at the same time. NLP gives your chatbot the wings to fly when it can't just walk and run.

Chatbots for a common person are nothing but a way to communicate with some intelligent machine at the other end. This machine can be either voice-based or text-based, where the user will provide input in their own language, which in computer science is generally called natural language.

We know that there is no black box that does the magic, and everything works just fine. One should know that there is nothing artificial in AI; it's actually machine learning and deep learning algorithms written by great people, running under the hood. Machines haven't reached a stage where they can think as similar as humans to have their own intelligence. AI systems today—what they do and the way they behave—are the outcome of how we have trained them.

So, to understand the natural language of the user in whatsoever language it may be, or whatever input form it may be (text, voice, image, etc.), we have to write algorithms and use techniques of NLP. NLP is considered the brain of chatbots that processes the raw data, does the munging, cleans it, and then prepares to take appropriate actions.

NLP in itself is a huge topic and requires time and perseverance to learn completely, but there are few methods that are necessary for a chatbot developer to know, which we are going to learn in this chapter.

# What Is spaCy?

spaCy is an open-source software library for advanced NLP, written in Python and Cython, built by Matthew Honnibal. It provides intuitive APIs to access its methods trained by deep learning models.

spaCy offers the fastest syntactic parser in the world. Taken directly from spaCy's documentation, they have some amazing benchmarking results, which are shown below.

## Benchmarks Results of spaCy

Two peer-reviewed papers in 2015 confirmed that spaCy offers the fastest syntactic parser in the world and that its accuracy is within 1% of the best available. The few systems that are more accurate are 20 times slower or more. Lets try to look at Figure 2-1 which shows spaCy benchmarking results based on its speed and accuracy compared to other libraries.

| SYSTEM | YEAR | LANGUAGE | ACCURACY | SPEED (WPS) |
|---|---|---|---|---|
| **spaCy v2.x** | 2017 | Python / Cython | **92.6** | n/a ⑦ |
| **spaCy v1.x** | 2015 | Python / Cython | 91.8 | 13,963 |
| ClearNLP | 2015 | Java | 91.7 | 10,271 |
| CoreNLP | 2015 | Java | 89.6 | 8,602 |
| MATE | 2015 | Java | 92.5 | 550 |
| Turbo | 2015 | C++ | 92.4 | 349 |

***Figure 2-1.*** *spaCy benchmarking results*

spaCy also offers statistical neural network models for a wide range of languages like English, German, Spanish, Portuguese, French, Italian, Dutch, and multi-language NER. It also provides tokenization for various other languages. This table shows speed benchmarked by Choi et al., so it wouldn't be fair to compare spaCy v2.x benchmarked on different hardware. This is the reason you do not see the speed column value for spaCy v2.x.

# What Does spaCy Provide?

There are three primary things that spaCy claims to provide and with which it is extremely helpful. Let's try to look at those and understand why one should know and use spaCy as a go-to module for doing NLP.

## World's Fastest Library

spaCy does extremely well at extracting large-scale information. It is written from scratch with utmost care for memory with help of the Cython library.

## Get Things Done

spaCy is designed with "get things done" in mind. It helps us in accomplishing real-world NLP scenarios. The clean documentation saves a lot of time for developers and computational linguistics enthusiasts and makes them more productive. It's easy to install, just like any other Python package.

## Deep Learning

spaCy is one of the best libraries available in the open-source community to process text for deep-learning algorithms. It collaborates seamlessly with TensorFlow, PyTorch, scikit-learn, Gensim, and the rest of Python's related technologies. Deep learning developers can easily construct linguistically sophisticated statistical models for a range of NLP/NLU problems.

# Features of spaCy

No other NLP library provides an extremely wide range of APIs to do almost everything, which is what spaCy does. The best things about this library is it is continuously evolving and getting better and better. Let's have a sneak peek at the features of spaCy as mentioned on their official website [`https://spacy.io/`].

- Non-destructive tokenization

- Named entity recognition

- Support for 28+ languages

- 13 statistical models for 8 languages

- Pre-trained word vectors

- Easy deep-learning integration

- Part-of-speech tagging

- Labeled dependency parsing

- Syntax-driven sentence segmentation

- Built-in visualizers for syntax and NER

- Convenient string-to-hash mapping

- Export to numpy data arrays

- Efficient binary serialization

- Easy model packaging and deployment

- State-of-the-art speed

- Robust, rigorously evaluated accuracy

Now, let's dive into this awesome module for NLP in Python: spaCy.

# Installation and Prerequisites

Before we actually dive into spaCy and code snippets, make sure you have Python installed on your OS. If not, refer to [1].

You can use whichever version of Python you are comfortable with. Most of the systems today come pre-installed with default Python version 2.7.x. We'll be using Python 3 in this chapter. So, if you want to use Python 3, please install Python 3 on your operating system by downloading it from `https://www.python.org/downloads/`. If you have Python 2 installed already, you can use that as well; it may or may not need minor code changes.

We will install spaCy via pip [2].

We are going to use a virtual environment [3] and install spaCy into a user directory.

If you are on macOS/OSX/Linux, follow these steps:

```
Step 1: python3 -m pip install -U virtualenv
Step 2: virtualenv venv -p /usr/local/bin/python3 #Make sure you use your
        own OS path for python 3 executable.
Step 3: source venv/bin/activate
Step 4: pip3 install -U spacy # We'll be using spaCy version 2.0.11.
```

The final step may take time, so wait patiently.

If you are on Windows ,just change the Step 3 to

```
venv\Scripts\activate
```

Now, we are going to install *Jupyter Notebook* inside our virtual environment, which we activated in the Step 3. Using *Jupyter Notebook* is much easier and more productive than standard Python interpreter. We will be executing all the snippets in Jupyter Notebook in the coming chapters.

To install Jupyter Notebook, run the following pip command:

```
pip3 install jupyter
```

This command will install Jupyter Notebook in your system.

At this point you should have spaCy and Jupyter Notebook installed in your virtualenv. Let's verify if everything was successfully installed.

1.  Go to your command line interface and type the following and
    you should see a server being started and opening a url in your
    default browser.

    ```
    $ jupyter notebook
    ```

    The default url is http://localhost:8888/tree. It should look
    something like Figure 2-2.

2.  Click on New as shown in Figure 2-2, and choose Python 3.
    It will open a new tab in your current browser and create a new
    notebook for you, where you can play with the Python code.
    You can execute any Python code, import libraries, plot charts,
    and markdown cells.

**Figure 2-2.** *Jupyter Notebook first look*

3.  Type import spaCy and run the cell by clicking on "Run" button or by pressing Shift + Enter. It should look something like Figure 2-3.

**Figure 2-3.** *Verifying spaCy installation*

If Step 3 doesn't throw any error messages, then you have successfully installed the spaCy module on your system. You should see your installed spaCy version in your notebook. If you want to install the same version of spaCy then you can specify the version while installing spaCy via pip.

```
pip3 install -U spacy==2.0.11
```

# What Are SpaCy Models?

SpaCy models are just like any other machine learning or deep learning models. A model is a yield of an algorithm or, say, an object that is created after training data using a machine learning algorithm. spaCy has lots of such models that can be placed directly in our program by downloading it just like any other Python package.

Now, we are going to install spaCy models as Python packages.

To do that, we'll run the following command in the notebook by taking use of notebook's magic command. By prefixing! [Exclamation Operator] before the shell command, we can run shell commands as well from Jupyter Notebooks. Let's see how it looks.

```
!python3 -m spacy download en
```

You might get a permission issue while using Jupyter Notebook to download spaCy models for Python 3. Go to your terminal and run the following command:

```
sudo python3 -m download en
```

See Figure 2-4 for reference.

```
Sumit:Chapter II geospark-device-3$ sudo python3 -m spacy download en
Password:
Collecting https://github.com/explosion/spacy-models/releases/download/en_core_web_sm-2.0.0/(
  Downloading https://github.com/explosion/spacy-models/releases/download/en_core_web_sm-2.0.
    100% |████████████████████████████████| 37.4MB 59.0MB/s
Requirement already satisfied (use --upgrade to upgrade): en-core-web-sm==2.0.0 from https:/,
eb_sm-2.0.0/en_core_web_sm-2.0.0.tar.gz in /usr/local/lib/python3.6/site-packages
You are using pip version 10.0.1, however version 18.0 is available.
You should consider upgrading via the 'pip install --upgrade pip' command.


    /usr/local/lib/python3.6/site-packages/en_core_web_sm -->
    /usr/local/lib/python3.6/site-packages/spacy/data/en

    You can now load the model via spacy.load('en')
```

***Figure 2-4.*** *Downloading spaCy models*

As you can see in Figure 2-4, spaCy tries to download some core files and installs them as Python packages.

---

**Note**    ! [Exclamation Operator] works only in Jupyter Notebook. To install spaCy models directly from the terminal, you need to remove! [Exclamation Operator]; otherwise it will result into an error.

---

[1]   https://www.python.org/downloads/

[2]   https://packaging.python.org/tutorials/installing-packages/#installing-from-pypi

[3]   http://docs.python-guide.org/en/latest/dev/virtualenvs/

# Fundamental Methods of NLP for Building Chatbots

It's really important to be good at basics to be an expert at something and do it effectively and efficiently. To build chatbots, we need to know the fundamental methods of NLP. These methods help us break the input into chunks and make sense of it. In the next section, we are going to learn some of the most used NLP methods that will not just help you be good at NLP but also good at building cool chatbots. The more we can process the input text better and more efficiently, the better we can respond to the user.

## POS Tagging

Part-of-speech (POS) tagging is a process where you read some text and assign parts of speech to each word or token, such as noun, verb, adjective, etc.

POS tagging becomes extremely important when you want to identify some entity in a given sentence. The first step is to do POS tagging and see what our text contains.

Let's get our hands dirty with some of the examples of real POS tagging.

**Example 1:**

```
nlp = spacy.load('en') #Loads the spacy en model into a python object
doc = nlp(u'I am learning how to build chatbots') #Creates a doc object
for token in doc:
    print(token.text, token.pos_) #prints the text and POS
```

**Output:**

```
('I', 'PRON')
('am', 'VERB')
('learning', 'VERB')
('how', 'ADV')
('to', 'PART')
('build', 'VERB')
('chatbots', 'NOUN')
```

**Example 2:**

```
doc = nlp(u'I am going to London next week for a meeting.')
for token in doc:
    print(token.text, token.pos_)
```

**Output:**

```
('I', 'PRON')
('am', 'VERB')
('going', 'VERB')
('to', 'ADP')
('London', 'PROPN')
('next', 'ADJ')
('week', 'NOUN')
('for', 'ADP')
('a', 'DET')
('meeting', 'NOUN')
('.', 'PUNCT')
```

As we can see, when we print the tokens from the returned Doc object from the method nlp, which is a container for accessing the annotations, we get the POS tagged with each of the words in the sentence.

These tags are the properties belonging to the word that determine the word is used in a grammatically correct sentence. We can use these tags as the word features in information filtering, etc.

Let's try to take another example where we try to explore different attributes of the token coming from Doc object.

**Example 3:**

```
doc = nlp(u'Google release "Move Mirror" AI experiment that matches your
pose from 80,000 images')

    for token in doc:
        print(token.text, token.lemma_, token.pos_, token.tag_, token.dep_,
            token.shape_, token.is_alpha, token.is_stop)
```

**Output:**

| Text | Lemma | POS | Tag | Dep | Shape | Alpha | Stop |
|------|-------|-----|-----|-----|-------|-------|------|
| **Google** | google | PROPN | NNP | compound | Xxxxx | True | False |
| **Release** | release | NOUN | NN | nmod | xxxx | True | False |
| **"** | " | PUNCT | `` | punct | " | False | False |
| **Move** | move | PROPN | NNP | nmod | Xxxx | True | False |
| **Mirror** | mirror | PROPN | NNP | nmod | Xxxxx | True | False |
| **"** | " | PUNCT | " | punct | " | False | False |
| **AI** | ai | PROPN | NNP | compound | XX | True | False |
| **Experiment** | experiment | NOUN | NN | ROOT | xxxx | True | False |
| **That** | that | ADJ | WDT | nsubj | xxxx | True | True |
| **Matches** | match | VERB | VBZ | relcl | xxxx | True | False |
| **Your** | -PRON- | ADJ | PRP$ | poss | xxxx | True | True |
| **Pose** | pose | NOUN | NN | dobj | xxxx | True | False |
| **From** | from | ADP | IN | prep | xxxx | True | True |
| **80,000** | 80,000 | NUM | CD | nummod | dd,ddd | False | False |
| **Images** | image | NOUN | NNS | pobj | xxxx | True | False |

**Example 4:**

```
doc = nlp(u'I am learning how to build chatbots')
for token in doc:
    print(token.text, token.lemma_, token.pos_, token.tag_, token.dep_,
        token.shape_, token.is_alpha, token.is_stop)
```

39

**Output:**

| TEXT | LEMMA | POS | TAG | DEP | SHAPE | ALPHA | STOP |
|------|-------|-----|-----|-----|-------|-------|------|
| **I** | -PRON- | PRON | PRP | nsubj | X | True | False |
| **am** | be | VERB | VBP | aux | xx | True | True |
| **learning** | learn | VERB | VBG | ROOT | xxxx | True | False |
| **how** | how | ADV | WRB | advmod | xxx | True | True |
| **to** | to | PART | TO | aux | xx | True | True |
| **build** | build | VERB | VB | xcomp | xxxx | True | False |
| **chatbots** | chatbot | NOUN | NNS | dobj | xxxx | True | False |

Refer to the below table to find out the meaning of each attribute we printed in the code.

| TEXT | Actual text or word being processed |
|------|-------------------------------------|
| LEMMA | Root form of the word being processed |
| POS | Part-of-speech of the word |
| TAG | They express the part-of-speech (e.g., VERB) and some amount of morphological information (e.g., that the verb is past tense). |
| DEP | Syntactic dependency (i.e., the relation between tokens) |
| SHAPE | Shape of the word (e.g., the capitalization, punctuation, digits format) |
| ALPHA | Is the token an alpha character? |
| Stop | Is the word a stop word or part of a stop list? |

You can refer the below table to understand what each POS attribute values of the token object mean. This list gives a detailed idea of part-of-speech tags assigned by spaCy's models.

| POS | DESCRIPTION | EXAMPLES |
|---|---|---|
| ADJ | adjective | *big, old, green, incomprehensible, first* |
| ADP | adposition | *in, to, during* |
| ADV | adverb | *very, tomorrow, down, where, there* |
| AUX | auxiliary | *is, has (done), will (do), should (do)* |
| CONJ | conjunction | *and, or, but* |
| CCONJ | coordinating conjunction | *and, or, but* |
| DET | determiner | *a, an, the* |
| INTJ | interjection | *psst, ouch, bravo, hello* |
| NOUN | noun | *girl, cat, tree, air, beauty* |
| NUM | numeral | *1, 2017, one, seventy-seven, IV, MMXIV* |
| PART | particle | *'s, not,* |
| PRON | pronoun | *I, you, he, she, myself, themselves, somebody* |
| PROPN | proper noun | *Mary, John, London, NATO, HBO* |
| PUNCT | punctuation | *., (, ), ?* |
| SCONJ | subordinating conjunction | *if, while, that* |
| SYM | symbol | *$, %, §, ©, +, −, ×, ÷, =, :), ½* |
| VERB | verb | *run, runs, running, eat, ate, eating* |
| X | other | *sfpksdpsxmsa* |
| SPACE | space | |

So why is POS tagging needed for chatbots?

Answer: to reduce the complexity of understanding a text that can't be trained or is trained with less confidence. By use of POS tagging, we can identify parts of the text input and do string matching only for those parts. For example, if you were to find if a location exists in a sentence, then POS tagging would tag the location word as NOUN, so you can take all the NOUNs from the tagged list and see if it's one of the locations from your preset list or not.

# Stemming and Lemmatization

Stemming is the process of reducing inflected words to their word stem, base form.

A stemming algorithm reduces the words "saying" to the root word "say," whereas "presumably" becomes presum. As you can see, this may or may not always be 100% correct.

**Lemmatization** is closely related to **stemming**, but lemmatization is the algorithmic process of determining the lemma of a word based on its intended meaning.

For example, in English, the verb "to walk" may appear as "walk," "walked," "walks," or "walking." The base form, "walk," that one might look up in a dictionary, is called the *lemma* for the word. spaCy doesn't have any in-built stemmer, as lemmatization is considered more correct and productive.

Difference between Stemming and Lemmatization

- **Stemming** does the job in a crude, heuristic way that chops off the ends of words, assuming that the remaining word is what we are actually looking for, but it often includes the removal of derivational affixes.

- **Lemmatization** tries to do the job more elegantly with the use of a vocabulary and morphological analysis of words. It tries its best to remove inflectional endings only and return the dictionary form of a word, known as the lemma.

Though few libraries provide methods for stemming as well as lemmatization, it's always a best practice to use lemmatization to get the root word correctly.

Let's try to explore lemmatization by taking some of the examples:

**Example 1:**

```
from spacy.lemmatizer import Lemmatizer
from spacy.lang.en import LEMMA_INDEX, LEMMA_EXC, LEMMA_RULES
lemmatizer = Lemmatizer(LEMMA_INDEX, LEMMA_EXC, LEMMA_RULES)
lemmatizer('chuckles', 'NOUN') # 2nd param is token's part-of-speech tag
```

**Output:**

```
[u'chuckle']
```

**Example 2:**

```
lemmatizer('blazing', 'VERB')
```

**Output:**

```
[u'blaze']
```

**Example 3:**

```
lemmatizer('fastest', 'ADJ')
```

**Output:**

```
[u'fast']
```

If you want to see the comparison between a stemmer and lemmatizer, then you need to install one of the most popular libraries for Python: Natural Language Toolkit (NLTK). spaCy has gained popularity very recently, but it was NLTK that made every NLP enthusiast take a plunge into the ocean of NLP and its techniques.

Check the following example where we try to use two stemming techniques provided by NLTK. First, we try to get the stem of the word "fastest" using PorterStemmer and then using SnowBallStemmer. Both of them give the same result—that is, "fastest"— but when we do the lemmatization using spaCy's method, it gives us "fast" as the stem of "fastest," which is more meaningful and correct.

```
from nltk.stem.porter import *
from nltk.stem.snowball import SnowballStemmer
porter_stemmer = PorterStemmer()
snowball_stemmer = SnowballStemmer("english")
print(porter_stemmer.stem("fastest"))
print(snowball_stemmer.stem("fastest"))

fastest
fastest
```

---

**Note**   Make sure to install `nltk` package using pip3 before trying to run this code.

---

Since you are pretty much aware what a stemming or lemmatization does in NLP, you should be able to understand that whenever you come across a situation where you need the root form of the word, you need to do lemmatization there. For example, it is often used in building search engines. You must have wondered how Google gives you the articles in search results that you meant to get even when the search text was not properly formulated.

This is where one makes use of lemmatization. Imagine you search with the text, *"When will the next season of Game of Thrones be releasing?"*

Now, suppose the search engine does simple document word frequency matching to give you search results. In this case, the aforementioned query probably won't match an article with a caption *"Game of Thrones next season release date."*

If we do the lemmatization of the original question before going to match the input with the documents, then we may get better results.

We'll try to test this theory as well in upcoming sections.

# Named-Entity Recognition

**Named-entity recognition** (**NER**), also known by other names like **entity identification** or **entity extraction**, is a process of finding and classifying named entities existing in the given text into pre-defined categories.

The NER task is hugely dependent on the knowledge base used to train the NE extraction algorithm, so it may or may not work depending upon the provided dataset it was trained on.

spaCy comes with a very fast entity recognition model that is capable of identifying entity phrases from a given document. Entities can be of different types, such as person, location, organization, dates, numerals, etc. These entities can be accessed through .ents property of the doc object.

Let's try to find named-entities by taking some examples with the help of spaCy's powerful NER tagging capability.

**Example 1:**

```
my_string = u"Google has its headquarters in Mountain View, California
having revenue amounted to 109.65 billion US dollars"
doc = nlp(my_string)

for ent in doc.ents:
    print(ent.text, ent.label_)
```

**Output:**

```
('Google', 'ORG')
('Mountain View', 'GPE')
('California', 'GPE')
('109.65 billion US dollars', 'MONEY')
```

We can see how beautifully and automagically the spaCy model could easily identify that the word **Google** as an **Organization, California** is a **Geopolitical entity**, and in the given sentence we are talking about **109.65 billion US dollars,** which is actually about money.

Let's try to explore some more examples.

**Example 2:**

```
my_string = u"Mark Zuckerberg born May 14, 1984 in New York is an American
technology entrepreneur and philanthropist best known for co-founding and
leading Facebook as its chairman and CEO."
doc = nlp(my_string)

for ent in doc.ents:
    print(ent.text, ent.label_)
```

**Output:**

```
('Mark Zuckerberg', 'PERSON')
('May 14, 1984', 'DATE')
('New York', 'GPE')
('American', 'NORP')
('Facebook', 'ORG')
```

**Example 3:**

```
my_string = u"I usually wake up at 9:00 AM. 90% of my daytime goes in
learning new things."
doc = nlp(my_string)
for ent in doc.ents:
    print(ent.text, ent.label_)
```

**Output:**

```
('9:00 AM', 'TIME')
('90%', 'PERCENT')
```

As you can see, the entity extractor can easily extract the time information from the given string. Also as you can see entity extractor not just tries to identify the number but also exact PERCENTAGE value.

As per the documentation by spaCy, models trained on the OntoNotes 5[1] corpus support the following entity types.

| TYPE | DESCRIPTION |
| --- | --- |
| PERSON | People, including fictional |
| NORP | Nationalities or religious or political groups |
| FAC | Buildings, airports, highways, bridges, etc. |
| ORG | Companies, agencies, institutions, etc. |
| GPE | Countries, cities, states |
| LOC | Non-GPE locations, mountain ranges, bodies of water |
| PRODUCT | Objects, vehicles, foods, etc. (not services) |
| EVENT | Named hurricanes, battles, wars, sports events, etc. |
| WORK_OF_ART | Titles of books, songs, etc. |
| LAW | Named documents made into laws |
| LANGUAGE | Any named language |
| DATE | Absolute or relative dates or periods |
| TIME | Times smaller than a day |
| PERCENT | Percentage, including "%" |
| MONEY | Monetary values, including unit |
| QUANTITY | Measurements, as of weight or distance |
| ORDINAL | "first," "second," etc. |
| CARDINAL | Numerals that do not fall under another type |

---

[1]https://catalog.ldc.upenn.edu/ldc2013t19

Whenever we intend to build a conversational agent or chatbot in simple terms, we always have a domain in mind. For example, we want the chatbot to book a doctor's appointment, order food, pay a bill, fill out a banking application, e-Commerce, etc. The chatbot could be solving a combination of these problems as well. By finding out the entity in the question, one can get a fair idea of the context in which the question was asked.

Let's try to understand this by taking an example of two sentences with similar words and different meanings.

```
my_string1 = u"Imagine Dragons are the best band."
my_string2 = u"Imagine dragons come and take over the city."

doc1 = nlp(my_string1)
doc2 = nlp(my_string2)

for ent in doc1.ents:
    print(ent.text, ent.label_)
```

The above for loop over doc1 object *gives an output:*

```
('Imagine Dragons', 'ORG')
```

Awesome, isn't it? It'll become more intriguing when you will come to realize that the entity recognizer doesn't recognize any entity in 2nd string. Run the following code and doc2 doesn't produce any output.

```
for ent in doc2.ents:
    print(ent.text, ent.label_)
```

Now, imagine you were to extract the context of the above two strings in a live environment. What would you do? With help of *Entity Extractor*, one can easily figure out the context of the statement and intelligently take the conversation further.

## Stop Words

Stop words are high-frequency words like *a, an, the, to* and *also* that we sometimes want to filter out of a document before further processing. Stop words usually have little lexical content and do not hold much of a meaning.

Below is a list of 25 semantically non-selective stop words that are common in Reuters-RCV1.

```
a     an    and    are    as    at    be    by    for
from   has   he    in    is    it    its    of    on
that   the   to    was   were   will   with
```

*Let's get into some code and try to understand how things work.*

To see all the words defined as stop words in spaCy you can run the following lines of code:

```
from spacy.lang.en.stop_words import STOP_WORDS
print(STOP_WORDS)
```

*You should see something like:*

```
set(['all', 'six', 'just', 'less', 'being', 'indeed', 'over', 'move',
'anyway', 'fifty', 'four', 'not', 'own', 'through', 'using', 'go', 'only',
'its', 'before', 'one', 'whose', 'how',
.............................................................
.............................................................
.............................................................
.............................................................
'whereby', 'third', 'i', 'whole', 'noone', 'sometimes', 'well', 'together',
'yours', 'their', 'rather', 'without', 'so', 'five', 'the', 'otherwise',
'make', 'once'])
```

There are about 305 stop words defined in spaCy's stop words list. You can always define your own stop words if needed and override the existing list.

To see if a word is a stop word or not, you can use the nlp object of spaCy. We can use the nlp object's is_stop attribute.

**Example 1:**

```
nlp.vocab[u'is'].is_stop
```

**Output:**

```
True
```

**Example 2:**

```
nlp.vocab[u'hello'].is_stop
```

**Output:**

```
False
```

**Example 3:**

```
nlp.vocab[u'with'].is_stop
```

**Output:**

```
True
```

Stop words are a very important part of text clean up. It helps removal of meaningless data before we try to do actual processing to make sense of the text.

Suppose you are in a situation where you are building a bot to make people happy by assessing their mood. Now, one needs to analyze the sentiment in the text input by the user so that correct response can be formulated. Here, before begging to do basic sentiment analysis, we should remove the noise in the data that exists in the form of stop words.

# Dependency Parsing

Dependency parsing is one of the more beautiful and powerful features of spaCy that is fast and accurate. The parser can also be used for sentence boundary detection and lets you iterate over base noun phrases, or "chunks."

This feature of spaCy gives you a parsed tree that explains the parent-child relationship between the words or phrases and is independent of the order in which words occur.

Let's take an example where you have to parse the following sentence:
*Book me a flight from Bangalore to Goa*

**Example 1:**

```
doc = nlp(u'Book me a flight from Bangalore to Goa')
blr, goa = doc[5], doc[7]
list(blr.ancestors)
```

**Output:**

```
[from, flight, Book]
```

The above output can tell us that user is looking to book the flight from Bangalore.

Let's try to list the ancestors of goa.ancestors object:

```
list(goa.ancestors)
```

**Output:**

```
[to, flight, Book]
```

This output can tell us that the user is looking to book the flight to Goa.

# What Are Ancestors in Dependency Parsing?

Ancestors are the rightmost token of this token's syntactic descendants. Like in the above example for the object blr the ancestors were *from, flight,* and *Book.*

Remember you can always list the ancestors of a doc object item using ancestors attribute.

```
list(doc[4].ancestors) #doc[4]==flight
```

The above code will output:

```
[flight, Book]
```

To check if a doc object item is an ancestor of another *doc* object item programmatically, we can do the following:

```
doc[3].is_ancestor(doc[5])
```

The above returns True because doc[3] (i.e., flight) is an ancestor of doc[5] (i.e., Bangalore). You can try more examples like this to get a better understanding of dependency parsing and the ancestors concept.

If we try to think of a real-world scenario that we might actually face while trying to build a chatbot, we may come across some sentence like

*I want to book a cab to the hotel and a table at a restaurant.*

In this sentence, it's important to know what *tasks* are requested and where they are targeted (i.e., *whether the user wants to book a cab to the hotel or the restaurant*).

*Let's try to do that using the following code:*

**Example 1:**

```
doc = nlp(u'Book a table at the restaurant and the taxi to the hotel')
tasks = doc[2], doc[8] #(table, taxi)
tasks_target = doc[5], doc[11] #(restaurant, hotel)

for task in tasks_target:
        for tok in task.ancestors:
            if tok in tasks:
                print("Booking of {} belongs to {}".format(tok, task))
        break
```

**Output:**

```
Booking of table belongs to restaurant
Booking of taxi belongs to hotel
```

## What Are Children in Dependency Parsing?

Children are immediate syntactic dependents of the token. We can see the children of a word by using children attribute just like we used ancestors.

```
list(doc[3].children)
```

will output

```
[a, from, to]
```

## Interactive Visualization for Dependency Parsing

It's very difficult to understand the complete dependency parsing concept for the first time. spaCy gives an extremely easy and interactive way to understand its dependency parsing. spaCy v2.0+ has a visualization module where we can pass a Doc or a list of Doc objects to displaCy and call serve method of displaCy to run the web server.

Figure 2-5 shows how the interactive visualization will look for dependency parsing.

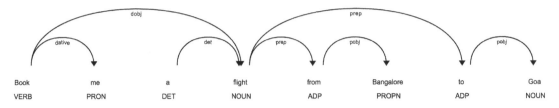

***Figure 2-5.*** *Interactive visualization for dependency parsing*

You can also generate the dependency parsing visualization in Figure 2-5. To create a visualization like this, run the following code and then go to `http://localhost:5000` in your browser.

Let's try to do the visualization of our example of tasks and the target of the tasks.

```
from spacy import displacy
doc = nlp(u'Book a table at the restaurant and the taxi to the hotel')
displacy.serve(doc, style='dep')
```

Running this code will have output like that in Figure 2-6. If you get something similar, then go to another tab of your browser and enter `http://localhost:5000`.

We get a visualization of dependency parsing for this string in the code (shown in Figure 2-7).

```
In [*]:  from spacy import displacy
         doc = nlp(u'Book a table at the restaurant and the taxi to the hotel')
         displacy.serve(doc, style='dep')

              Serving on port 5000...
              Using the 'dep' visualizer
```

***Figure 2-6.*** *Starting dependency parsing server on localhost*

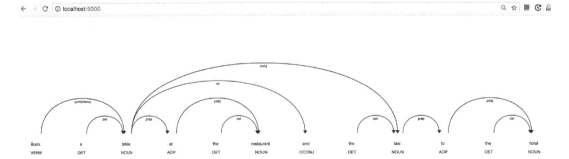

***Figure 2-7.*** *Example of dependency parsing*

Let's take one more example of dependency parsing where we assume a user is asking the following sentence:

*What are some places to visit in Berlin and stay in Lubeck?*

We will first create the doc object as shown here:

```
doc = nlp(u"What are some places to visit in Berlin and stay in Lubeck")
```

Now, we get the places being talked about and the actions the user wants:

```
places = [doc[7], doc[11]] #[Berlin, Lubeck]
actions = [doc[5], doc[9]] #[visit, stay]
```

Since you already know POS tagging and entity extraction, you can easily get the places and actions automatically.

Now that we have the places, let's iterate through each of its ancestors and check if any ancestors are found in actions. The first parent of place found in the list of actions should be the action for the place in question.

```
for place in places:
    for tok in place.ancestors:
        if tok in actions:
            print("User is referring {} to {}").format(place, tok)
            break
```

**Output:**

```
User is referring: Berlin to visit
User is referring: Lubeck to stay
```

As we see in these examples, dependency parsing makes it quite easy to understand what the user is referring to. We saw that in the case of two different tasks as well, we can pretty figure out the expectation and, based on that, formulate the next response.

## What Is the Use of Dependency Parsing in Chatbots?

Dependency parsing is one the most important parts when building chatbots from scratch. It becomes far more important when you want to figure out the meaning of a text input from your user to your chatbot. There can be cases when you haven't trained your chatbots, but still you don't want to lose your customer or reply like a dumb machine.

In these cases, dependency parsing really helps to find the relation and explain a bit more about what the user may be asking for.

If we were to list things for which dependency parsing helps, some might be:

- It helps in finding relationships between words of grammatically correct sentences.

- It can be used for sentence boundary detection.

- It is quite useful to find out if the user is talking about more than one context simultaneously.

You must be wondering, what if your bot user says any grammatically incorrect sentence or uses any SMS textspeak while giving input about something? As discussed in Chapter 1, you have to be cautious about these situations and handle them accordingly using NLP techniques.

You need to write your own custom NLP to understand the context of the user or your chatbot and, based on that, identify the possible grammatical mistakes a user can make.

All in all, you must be ready for such scenarios where a user will input garbage values or grammatically incorrect sentences. You can't handle all such scenarios at once, but you can keep improving your chatbot by adding custom NLP code or by limiting user input by design.

# Noun Chunks

Noun chunks or NP-chunking are basically "base noun phrases." We can say they are flat phrases that have a noun as their head. You can think of noun chunks as a noun with the words describing the noun.

Let's try to take an example and understand it better.

**Example 1:**

```
doc = nlp(u"Boston Dynamics is gearing up to produce thousands of robot
dogs")
list(doc.noun_chunks)
```

**Output:**

```
[Boston Dynamics, thousands, robot dogs]
```

Though having noun chunks from a given sentence helps a lot, spaCy provides other attributes that can be helpful too. Let's try to explore some of those.

**Example 2:**

```
doc = nlp(u"Deep learning cracks the code of messenger RNAs and protein-
coding potential")
for chunk in doc.noun_chunks:
    print(chunk.text, chunk.root.text, chunk.root.dep_,
          chunk.root.head.text)
```

**Output:**

| TEXT | ROOT.TEXT | ROOT.DEP_ | ROOT.HEAD.TEXT |
|---|---|---|---|
| **deep learning** | learning | nsubj | cracks |
| **the code** | code | dobj | cracks |
| **messenger RNAs** | RNAs | pobj | of |
| **protein-coding potential** | potential | conj | RNAs |

As we can see from this table we get the noun chunks and their attributes. The following table will help you understand each column.

| Column | Meaning |
|---|---|
| **Text** | Text of the original noun chunk |
| **Root text** | Text of the original word that connects the noun chunk with remaining parse |
| **Root dep** | Dependency relation that connects the root to its head |
| **Root head text** | Text of the root token's head |

# Finding Similarity

Finding similarity between two words is a use-case you will find most of the time working with NLP. Sometimes it becomes fairly important to find if two words are similar. While building chatbots you will often come to situations where you don't have to just find similar-looking words but also how closely related two words are logically.

spaCy uses high-quality word vectors to find similarity between two words using *GloVe algorithm* (Global Vectors for Word Representation).

GloVe is an unsupervised learning algorithm for obtaining vector representations for words. GloVe algorithm uses aggregated global word-word co-occurrence statistics from a corpus to train the model.

Let's try to look at the actual values inside the vectors of spaCy using *vector* attribute of the token.

```
doc = nlp(u'How are you doing today?')
for token in doc:
    print(token.text, token.vector[:5])
```

**Output:**

```
(u'How', array([-0.29742685,  0.73939574,
-0.04001453,  0.44034013,  2.8967502 ],       dtype=float32))
(u'are', array([-0.23435134, -1.6145049 ,  1.0197453 ,  0.9928169 ,
  0.28227055],       dtype=float32))(u'you', array([ 0.10252178,
-3.564711  ,  2.4822793 ,  4.2824993 ,  3.590245  ],       dtype=float32))
(u'doing', array([-0.6240922 , -2.0210216 , -0.91014993,  2.7051923 ,
  4.189252  ],       dtype=float32))(u'today', array([ 3.5409122 ,
-0.62185854,  2.6274266 ,  2.0504875 ,  0.20191991],       dtype=float32))
(u'?', array([ 2.8914998 , -0.25079122,  3.3764176 ,  1.6942682 ,
  1.9849057 ],       dtype=float32))
```

Seeing this output, it doesn't make much sense and meaning. From an application's perspective, what matters the most is how similar the vectors of different words are—that is, the word's meaning itself.

In order to find similarity between two words in spaCy, we can do the following.

**Example 1:**

```
hello_doc = nlp(u"hello")
hi_doc = nlp(u"hi")
hella_doc = nlp(u"hella")
print(hello_doc.similarity(hi_doc))
print(hello_doc.similarity(hella_doc))
```

**Output:**

```
0.7879069442766685
0.4193425861242359
```

If you see the word *hello,* it is more related and similar to the word *hi,* even though there is only a difference of a character between the words *hello* and *hella.*

*Let's take one more example of a sentence and learn how spaCy does the similarity comparison. Remember our Game of Thrones example in previous sections? We are going to try that and see the similarity.*

**Code:**

```
GoT_str1 = nlp(u"When will next season of Game of Thrones be releasing?")
GoT_str2 = nlp(u"Game of Thrones next season release date?")
GoT_str1.similarity(GoT_str2)
```

**Output:**

```
0.785019122782813
```

As we can see in this example, the similarity between both of the sentences is about 79%, which is good enough to say that both of the sentences are quite similar, which is true. This can help us save a lot of time for writing custom code when building chatbots. So, we come to a fact that spaCy gives us a meaningful similarity between two words using the word vectors rather than just looking at their spelling or alphabets.

We will take a very simple example and try to find the similarity between words.

```
example_doc = nlp(u"car truck google")

for t1 in example_doc:
    for t2 in example_doc:
        similarity_perc = int(t1.similarity(t2) * 100)
        print "Word {} is {}% similar to word {}".format(t1.text,
        similarity_perc,  t2.text)
```

**Output:**

```
Word car is 100% similar to word car
Word car is 71% similar to word truck
Word car is 24% similar to word google
Word truck is 71% similar to word car
Word truck is 100% similar to word truck
Word truck is 36% similar to word google
Word google is 24% similar to word car
Word google is 36% similar to word truck
Word google is 100% similar to word google
```

Finding similarity between words or sentences becomes quite important when we intend to build any application that is hugely dependent on the implementations of NLP. If you have ever used StackOverflow, whenever we try to ask a new question, it tries to list similar questions already asked on the platform. This is one of the best examples where finding similarity between two sets of sentences might help. spaCy's confidence to find the similarity between two words based on an already trained model purely depends on the kind of general assumption taken.

When building chatbots, finding similarity can be very handy for the following situations:

- When building chatbots for recommendation
- Removing duplicates
- Building a spell-checker

These things that we learned are really important while building chatbots so that we know how to parse user inputs so that they make sense while writing business logic inside code.

# Good to Know Things in NLP for Chatbots

In this section we are going to learn about a couple of interesting topics that come in handy often when you plan to write your own custom NLP methods to handle certain scenarios. Make sure you go through them, as when you expect it the least, it's needed the most. We will briefly talk about tokenization and usage of regular expressions in a chatbot scenario.

NATURAL LANGUAGE PROCESSING FOR CHATBOTS

# Tokenization

Tokenization is one of the simple yet basic concepts of NLP where we split a text into meaningful segments. spaCy first tokenizes the text (i.e., segments it into words and then punctuation and other things). A question might come to your mind: Why can't I just use the built-in *split* method of Python language and do the tokenization? Python's split method is just a raw method to split the sentence into tokens given a separator. It doesn't take any meaning into account, whereas tokenization tries to preserve the meaning as well.

Let's try some code and see how tokenization works.

**Example 1:**

```
doc = nlp(u'Brexit is the impending withdrawal of the U.K. from the
European Union.')
for token in doc:
    print(token.text)
```

**Output:**

```
Brexit
is
the
impending
withdrawal
of
the
U.K.
from
the
EuropeanUnion
```

If you see in the above output, U.K. comes as a single word after the tokenization process, which makes sense, as U.K. is a country name and splitting it would be wrong. Even after this if you not happy with spaCy's tokenization, then you can use its `add_special_case` case method to add your own rule before relying completely on spaCy's tokenization method.

# Regular Expressions

You must already know about regular expressions and their usage. This book assumes you must be familiar with regular expressions in general. In this section, we are just going to run through some of the examples and see how regular expressions can be beneficial and useful while building chatbots.

Text analysis and processing is a big subject in itself. Sometimes words play together in a way that makes it extremely difficult for machines to understand and get trained upon.

Regular expression can come handy for some fallback for a machine learning model. It has the power of pattern-matching, which can ensure that the data we are processing is correct or incorrect. Most of the early chatbots discussed in Chapter 1 under the History of Chatbots section were hugely dependent on pattern-matching.

Let's take below two examples that are pretty simple to understand. We'll try to use regular expression to extract information from both of the sentences.

Book me a metro from Airport Station to Hong Kong Station.

Book me a cab from Hong Kong Airport to AsiaWorld-Expo.

Here is the code:

```
sentence1 = "Book me a metro from Airport Station to Hong Kong Station."
sentence2 = "Book me a cab to Hong Kong Airport from AsiaWorld-Expo."

import re
from_to = re.compile('.* from (.*) to (.*)')
to_from = re.compile('.* to (.*) from (.*)')

from_to_match = from_to.match(sentence2)
to_from_match = to_from.match(sentence2)

if from_to_match and from_to_match.groups():
    _from = from_to_match.groups()[0]
    _to = from_to_match.groups()[1]
    print("from_to pattern matched correctly. Printing values\n")
    print("From: {}, To: {}".format(_from, _to))

elif to_from_match and to_from_match.groups():
    _to = to_from_match.groups()[0]
    _from = to_from_match.groups()[1]
```

```
print("to_from pattern matched correctly. Printing values\n")
print("From: {}, To: {}".format(_from, _to))
```

**Output:**

```
to_from pattern matched correctly. Printing values
From: AsiaWorld-Expo., To: Hong Kong Airport
```

Try changing the sentence2 to sentence1 and see if the code works well to identify the pattern. Given the power of machine learning these days, regular expression and pattern-matching has taken a back step, but make sure you brush up a bit about it as it may be needed at any time to parse specific details from words, sentences, or text documents.

# Summary

At this point you must have fair idea of why we need to know NLP before starting to build chatbots. In this chapter, we learned about the spaCy module in Python, its features, and how to install it. We dived into various methods of NLP, which is extensively used while building chatbots. We learned about POS tagging, the difference between stemming and lemmatization, entity recognition, noun-chunking, and finding similarity between sets of words.

We executed code for all of these concepts and learned all of this by doing and not just reading, which is what this book emphasizes. We brushed up on basics of tokenization and regular expressions as well. We are good to go on and build our chatbot in the next chapter using a freely available tool called Dialogflow. We will learn how to train our chatbot to understand and extract information given by the user in the next chapter.

# CHAPTER 3

# Building Chatbots the Easy Way

Building chatbots the easy way has been written keeping in mind that sometimes you don't want to build everything from scratch and just want to get things done. This chapter doesn't require you to do lots of coding but still gives you a fair idea of how to build chatbots in an easy way and make it public.

The reason why this chapter becomes more important for learning to build chatbots is because the software world moves too fast to be adapted. Sometimes we need to build applications very quickly, and we try to look for tools available in open-source libraries that can be used to quickly build applications, without the need of re-inventing the wheels. Sometimes we are not good enough at coding to build everything from scratch. Even though we want to build applications from scratch, we can't because the learning curve will be so steep for a newbie.

This chapter will help you to build chatbots very quickly and make them public for the world to use.

We are going to try a tool formerly known as Api.ai. Now it is known as Dialogflow.

## Introduction to Dialogflow

Dialogflow gives users new methods to interact with their product by building engaging voice- and text-based conversational interfaces, such as voice apps and chatbots. Dialogflow is powered by AI. It helps you connect with users on your website, mobile app, the Google Assistant, Amazon Alexa, Facebook Messenger, and other popular platforms and devices.

The following diagram from Dialogflow shows how they handle a user request.

© Sumit Raj 2019
S. Raj, *Building Chatbots with Python*, https://doi.org/10.1007/978-1-4842-4096-0_3

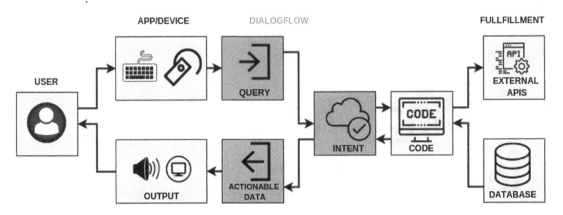

*Figure 3-1.* *Working diagram of Dialogflow architecture*

Here is what happens:

1. User talks to the input device.

2. User query goes into the Dialogflow engine.

3. Dialogflow tries to recognize the intent.

4. Based on the intent, a fulfillment is done and data is returned from database.

5. Response is returned to the intent.

6. Response is converted into actionable data.

7. User's request for information is given back to the output device.

There is a concept of agents in Dialogflow that are best described as Natural Language Understanding (NLU) modules. These can be included in your app, product, or service and transform natural user requests into actionable data. This transformation occurs when a user input matches one of the intents inside your agent.

Agents can also be designed to manage a conversation flow in a specific way. This can be done with the help of contexts, intent priorities, slot filling, responsibilities, and fulfillment via webhook.

# Getting Started

Knowing what we have learned so far was and is important because free tools and packages available in open source don't always help in building a full-fledged chatbot application.

Many times, you may come across a situation when you want to build everything yourself so that you have more control over your application. We will learn those in the next chapter and use the previously learned NLP techniques as well.

This chapter is all about creating a chatbot as a proof of concept and making it ready for the world to use with minimal programming or no programming experience.

# Building a Food-Ordering Chatbot

We are going to create a chatbot with help of Dialogflow for a specific restaurant. Let's name it **OnlineEatsBot**. In short we can call it OnlineEats product. You can choose any other use-case for which you want to build the chatbot. For this chapter we are going to build a food-ordering chatbot.

# Deciding the Scope

Let's decide the scope of this chatbot—that is, what it can do and to what extent.

- It should be able to greet the user dynamically.

- It should be able to understand the menu items and their quantity requested.

- Chatbot should be able to place an order on the user's behalf.

- Give the user the status of the order when asked.

# Listing Intents

Here we list the intents we want our chatbot to train with so that it can understand those intents when asked by the user.

Intents

- Default welcome intent: when the user messages the chatbot

- Place order intent: when the user asks the bot to order food

- Item description intent: when the user tells what item and quantity they want

- Order status: when the user wants to know his order status

- Order_ID: the bot needs to understand the user's order ID for tracking.

- User thanks: when the user thanks the bot

# Listing Entities

We'll try to list all possible entities for all intents here. Later in the chapter we'll see them being defined for whichever intent they are applicable.

Entities

- food_items: what food does the user want to order?

- quantities: what is the quantity of the food item the user is willing to order?

- order_id: order_id of the place order for user

# Building a Food Ordering Chatbot

Let's also level-set the expectation of the chatbot in terms of the minimum things we should be able to see it doing. For that, let's create a script of a conversation between our chatbot and the user. This helps us to stick to the plan to getting a basic working chatbot ready, assuming the user is doing the conversation in a nice and correct manner.

Chatbot and User Conversation Script:

> **User:** Hello
>
> **OnlineEatsBot:** Hello and Welcome! How may I help you?
>
> **User:** I am looking to order Chinese food.
>
> **OnlineEatsBot:** Sure, what would you like to order today?
>
> **User:** One chicken dumpling and two spring rolls.
>
> **OnlineEatsBot:** Done. Your final amount is XYZ, and your order is placed for 1 Chicken dumpling and 2 spring rolls.
>
> **User:** I haven't received my order yet. Where is my food?
>
> **OnlineEatsBot:** Can you please help me with your order ID?
>
> **User:** 123456
>
> **OnlineEatsBot:** Order Status for Order ID: 123456. The delivery guy is in your locality, your food will arrive in about 5 minutes.
>
> **User:** Thanks.
>
> **OnlineEatsBot:** Thanks a lot for your cooperation.

Now that we have written a basic script to follow to build our chatbot, we'll now dive into Dialogflow.

# Getting Started With Dialogflow

Let's follow these steps to create an account in Dialogflow and then create an agent. (An agent is nothing but another name for a chatbot.)

1. Create an account at `https://dialogflow.com`, and log in to the account.

2. Create an agent.

OnlineEatsBot|                                                    CREATE        ⋮

DEFAULT LANGUAGE ❓                          DEFAULT TIME ZONE

English — en                      ▼          (GMT+6:00) Asia/Almaty              ▼

Primary language for your agent. Other languages can be      Date and time requests are resolved using this timezone.
added later.

GOOGLE PROJECT

Create a new Google project                                                     ▼

Enables Cloud functions, Actions on Google and permissions management.

***Figure 3-2.*** *Creating a new agent in Dialogflow*

Enter the details, like name of the agent, time zone, default language, and Google Project that you want to choose or create a new Google project.

3. Create intents.

If you see Figure 3-3, you will see that we are given two intents already.

- **Default fallback intent:** Fallback intents are triggered if a user's input is not matched by any of the regular intents or enabled built-in small talk. When you create a new agent, a default fallback intent is created automatically. You can modify or delete it if you wish.

- **Default welcome intent:** We can extend this welcome intent for our own chatbots. You should add some of your own user expressions and default responses.

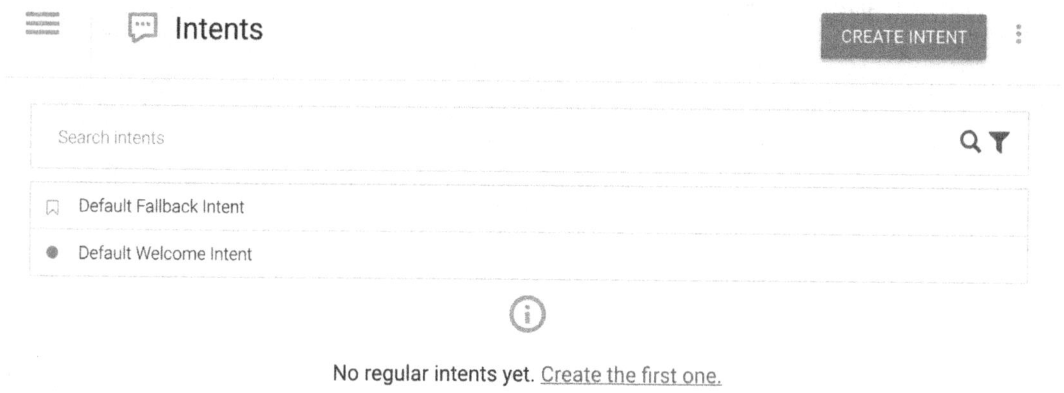

**Figure 3-3.** *Creating intents in Dialogflow*

Before we create our own intents, let's first add some utterances in default welcome intent and make it ready using the following steps:

1. Click on the default welcome intent.

2. Add your own user expressions in Training Phrases.

3. Click on **SAVE.**

When we click on save, the machine learning models behind the scenes run and train the data that we gave (i.e., the user expressions). Training the data means letting the machine understand what kind of intent it is based on the data that we provide and being able to predict when we give any new data to it. For example, if we look at Figure 3-4, where we have defined five user expressions that the machine already knows belong to "welcome intent," what if the user says "Hello there," which is not defined anywhere? The machine will still categorize "Hello there" as **default welcome intent**, as the features used in training and the machine for welcome intent are similar in the new user expression.

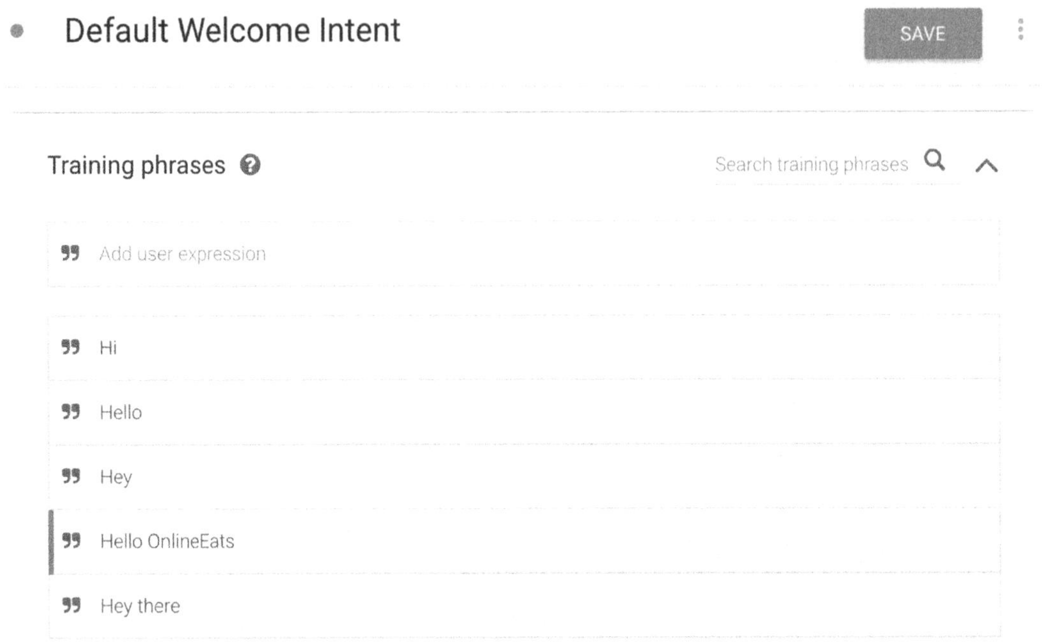

● **Default Welcome Intent**                                 SAVE   ⋮

---

Training phrases ❓                              Search training phrases 🔍 ∧

> 99   Add user expression

> 99   Hi

> 99   Hello

> 99   Hey

> 99   Hello OnlineEats

> 99   Hey there

*Figure 3-4.* *Defining a default welcome or greeting intent in Dialogflow*

Let's try to see if the welcome intent works for us. With Dialogflow we can do that in the dashboard itself. See Figure 3-5.

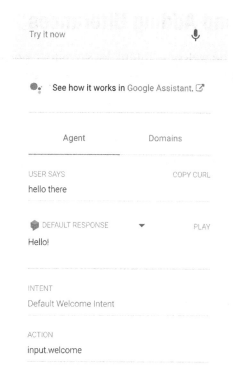

**Figure 3-5.**  *Testing the welcome intent in Dialogflow*

# Points to Remember When Creating Intents

Let's look at some of the points important to know while creating intents on Dialogflow.

- Dialogflow's intent also has the facility to have a default response of every intent. A default response is a response given back to the user every time that intent is recognized. In our example, when a user says "Hello there," we get "Hello!" as the response from the bot.

- If you want to you can add more responses or delete existing ones, having more than one response makes the bot look realistic so that it doesn't reply with the same response every time and feels human to the user talking to the bot.

- Intents in Dialogflow also have the capability of being marked as the end of the conversation. In other words, you can let the bot assume that the user will not be participating in the conversation anymore, and the bot can do the necessary action, based on this information, to end the conversation.

# Creating Intents and Adding Utterances

Now that we have created the welcome intent, let's create the **order intent**. I named it **place_order_intent**. The following are my user expressions that I entered:

*I want food*

*I want to order food asap*

*Can you please take my order for food?*

*Take my order please*

*I want to place an order for Chinese food*

*I want to place an order*

*Would you please help me to order food?*

*Can you please order food for me?*

*I want to order food*

*I am looking to order Thai food*

*I am looking to order Chinese food*

Now, we have built the intent to identify the aforementioned user expressions or related user expressions. Now, it's time to add a response back to the user using *default response* to the intent.

# Adding Default Response to the Intent

We'll be adding three possible responses that will be given back to the user once **place_order_intent** is encountered.

Sure, What would you like to order today?

Definitely, What would you like to have today?

Certainly, I'll try to help you with that. What are you feeling like eating today?

Now, the next step is to wait for the user to input the items he wants and parse the items.

Now we'll create a new intent that tells us what the user actually intends to order (i.e., the food items).

We create a new intent named **items_description**

First, we add our standard user expression.

*One chicken dumpling and two spring rolls.*

When we add the user expression then we can select specific words that we want to specify as entities of the intent. This could be quantity, date or time, location, etc., which are predefined, but we can create our own entities by clicking on the Create New button on the bottom right after we get the pop-up box.

Highlight the word in the utterance for which you want to make that selected word an entity. After that, it opens the pop-up box to create our own entity.

In this example, we should be able to parse the data in a nice readable format so that we can use that using any programming language. JSON format is the best format we can have in today's cross-platform applications. Dialogflow returns the data in JSON format by default, which can be parsed to look something like the following code. It's always suggested to keep your data as minimal as possible; don't overwhelm the API response by giving too much data. Remember all of these at scale cost money.

```
{
  "food_items": {
    "chicken dumpling": 1,
    "Spring rolls": 2
  }
}
```

## Item Description Intent and Belonging Entities

We can select One and Two and define them as @sys.number, which is nothing but the data type. We'll create a new entity called **food_items_entity** to identify food items.

If you look at Figure 3-6, you'll find that we have ENTITY named as **food_items_entity**, but when we select the words, then we name the parameters as **food_items_entity1** and **food_items_entity2**; this is similar for the food quantity, which is a number where we name the first and second parameters as **quantity1** and **quantity2**, respectively.

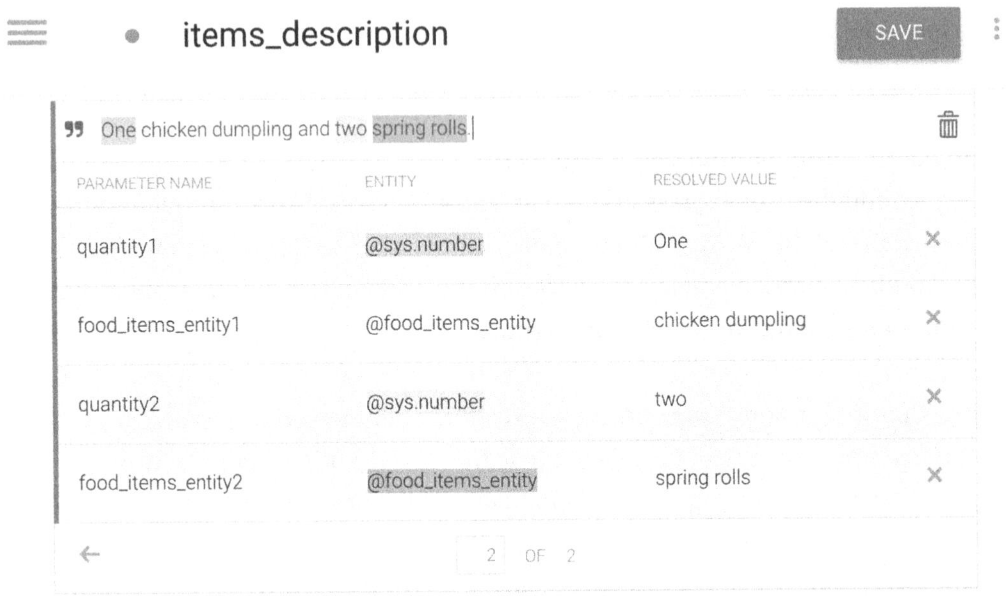

≡    ● items_description    SAVE    ⋮

> One chicken dumpling and two spring rolls.    🗑

| PARAMETER NAME | ENTITY | RESOLVED VALUE | |
| --- | --- | --- | --- |
| quantity1 | @sys.number | One | ✕ |
| food_items_entity1 | @food_items_entity | chicken dumpling | ✕ |
| quantity2 | @sys.number | two | ✕ |
| food_items_entity2 | @food_items_entity | spring rolls | ✕ |

← | 2 OF 2 |

*Figure 3-6. Item description intent*

What we define here will help us understand the JSON response, which we'll be getting after intent is triggered. We should have all these values there to move forward with the chatbot flow.

So, select the entire word or combination of words and click on Create New. A new screen will come to create entities; just enter the name for this new entity and save.

Now, come back to our intent for **items_description** and you should see something like Figure 3-6.

Keep adding more user expression in the training phrases, and keep defining the entities within it.

We have added four utterances so far, and this is how they look. We're going to add as many as possible so that our agent's accuracy for intent classification is better.

Dialogflow also has a feature to share the agent's training data. Training data used in this book can be accessed via Apress website, `https://github.com/Apress/building-chatbots-with-python`. As you can see in the Figure 3-7 where we try to add some more examples in the item description intent in our dialogflow agent.

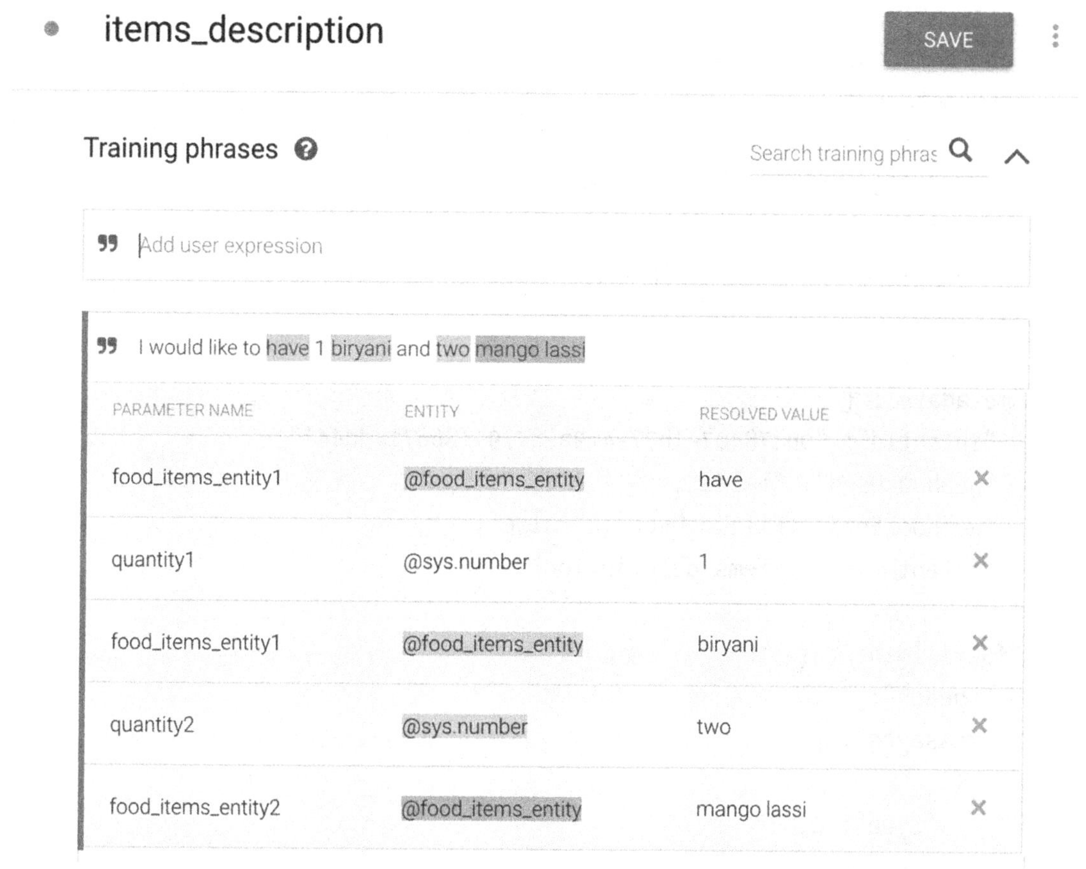

● **items_description**    SAVE    ⋮

Training phrases ❓                    Search training phras 🔍 ⌄

❝ |Add user expression

❝  I would like to have 1 biryani and two mango lassi

| PARAMETER NAME | ENTITY | RESOLVED VALUE | |
|---|---|---|---|
| food_items_entity1 | @food_items_entity | have | ✕ |
| quantity1 | @sys.number | 1 | ✕ |
| food_items_entity1 | @food_items_entity | biryani | ✕ |
| quantity2 | @sys.number | two | ✕ |
| food_items_entity2 | @food_items_entity | mango lassi | ✕ |

***Figure 3-7.*** *Adding more utterances in item description intent*

Now, at this point once we have saved our intent, and our agent has finished training the models. If we enter the following sentence on the right side, we should be able to see the following JSON response:

*One chicken dumpling and two spring rolls*

**Response from the intent:**

```
{
  "id": "e8cf4a44-6ec9-49ae-9da8-a5542a80d742",
  "timestamp": "2018-04-01T21:22:42.846Z",
  "lang": "en",
  "result": {
    "source": "agent",
    "resolvedQuery": "One chicken dumpling and two spring rolls",
```

```
    "action": "",
    "actionIncomplete": false,
    "parameters": {
      "quantity1": 1,
      "food_items_entity1": "chicken dumpling",
      "quantity2": 2,
      "food_items_entity2": "spring rolls"
    },
    "contexts": [],
    "metadata": {
      "intentId": "0b478407-1b37-4f9a-8779-1866714dd44f",
      "webhookUsed": "false",
      "webhookForSlotFillingUsed": "false",
      "intentName": "items_description"
    },
    "fulfillment": {
      "speech": "",
      "messages": [
        {
          "type": 0,
          "speech": ""
        }
      ]
    },
    "score": 1
  },
  "status": {
    "code": 200,
    "errorType": "success",
    "webhookTimedOut": false
  },
  "sessionId": "e1ee1860-06a7-4ca1-acae-f92c6e4a023e"
}
```

If you look at the *parameters* section of the JSON response we see

```
{
"quantity1": 1,
"food_items_entity1": "chicken dumpling",
"quantity2": 2,
"food_items_entity2": "spring rolls"
}
```

We can easily write some Python code to convert the JSON to our intended format we discussed.

---

### CAN YOU DO THIS?

Just test your Python skills and try to write a code that reads a JSON like the preceding and returns the quantity and food item belonging to it in another JSON format we discussed earlier.

---

# Understanding and Replying Back to the User

Now, next in the conversation is to make the bot reply back to the user that the order is understood along with any new information. New information could be the generated order_id, the order amount, or the expected delivery time. These things will be populated at your server end, and you can formulate it with the bot's response to give it back to the user.

Now, let's try to add the order amount in our case; to do that, we can use Dialogflow's **Default Response** feature and add this inside the intent. Let's hardcode the amount for now, as this amount will vary depending on the food items, their quantity, or the restaurant. Later in the chapter, we'll discuss how to make it dynamic by invoking an API.

The interesting thing here is that we can access the params we got from the intent (i.e., the food items and their quantities).

Responses can contain **references to parameter values**. We'll understand this in a moment.

If a parameter is present in the parameter table, we can use the following format to refer to its value in the 'Text response' field: $parameter_name.

We can use this params in the default response so that the bot confirms the order back to the user.

Add "*Done. Your final amount is XYZ and your order is placed for $quantity1 $food_items_entity1 and $quantity2 $food_items_entity2*" as the response.

---

**Note**    In case our intent is not able to parse the food items or their quantity, we need to give a different default response asking to explain what our bot couldn't understand or to at least confirm. We already learned how to add default response to an intent in the section "**Adding Default Response to the Intent**."

---

## Order Status Intent

Now, let's create the order_status intent, where the user may be trying to ask for the status of the order after the order is placed.

Figure 3-8 provides some training phrases we added for order status intent, and we name the intent **order_status**.

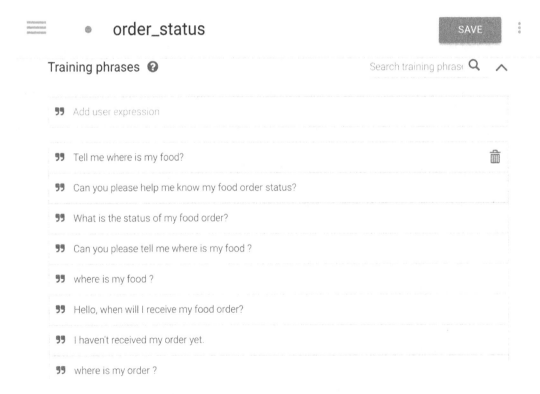

*Figure 3-8.*  *Creating order status intent*

Now, let's try some random order status asking utterances and see if our agent is intelligent enough to identify the intent.

I tried, *"Haven't received my food yet,"* and voila—my agent got it perfectly right that it's an **order_status** intent.

See the *resolvedQuery* and its intentName in the JSON in Figure 3-9.

## JSON

```
1 ▾ {
2       "id": "e68790f6-3d9c-4398-a7b1-5b1f6a3d0f1b",
3       "timestamp": "2018-04-01T21:45:20.386Z",
4       "lang": "en",
5 ▾     "result": {
6           "source": "agent",
7           "resolvedQuery": "Haven't received my food yet",
8           "action": "",
9           "actionIncomplete": false,
10          "parameters": {},
11          "contexts": [],
12 ▾        "metadata": {
13              "intentId": "a76ae537-b648-4e81-a03d-eca7bc84b136",
14              "webhookUsed": "false",
15              "webhookForSlotFillingUsed": "false",
16              "intentName": "order_status"
17          },
18 ▾        "fulfillment": {
19              "speech": "",
20 ▾            "messages": [
21 ▾                {
```

*Figure 3-9. JSON response from Dialogflow after query is resolved*

## User_Order_ID Intent

Now, next is to ask the user for Order ID, so let's set the default response of this intent to ask the following question.

*Can you please help me with your order ID?*

Now, the user will be giving their order ID, and our task is to identify that and give a response again.

So, for that we need to create another intent to identify when the user is talking about the order ID.

Note that the intents we are creating are pretty much independent of each other. In this case we know that the user is going to give the order ID, and it will mostly be right. If it's wrong you can always go back to the user and ask again.

We should also note that in some cases, order_id and phone number both may be integers. In such cases, we need to do some validation, like number of digits in order_id or phone number. Also, based on the context of the previous question, you can figure out if the user is giving an order_id or a phone number. As discussed in Chapter 1, we can always use decision trees for better flow management of the chatbot. Also we can programatically keep track that after **order_status** intent we ask for the order ID, and the user will be sending some order ID (some number), which is easier to parse in code rather than creating a new intent altogether.

In this example, we'll create user_order_id intent, as there is no conflict as such.

Now, we create a new intent called **user_order_id**

Figure 3-10 shows how our **user_order_id** intent looks.

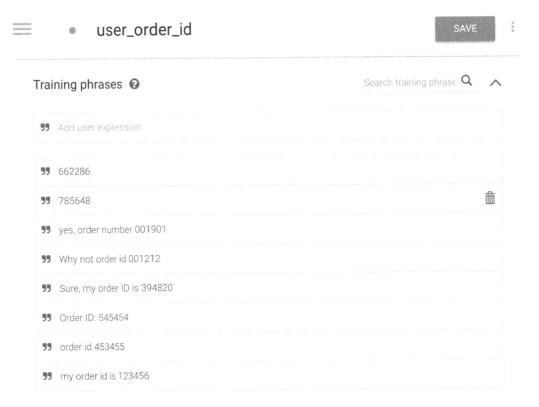

*Figure 3-10.* *Defining the user order ID intent in our agent*

I tested a couple of expressions, and it works well to classify them correctly as **user_order_id** intent. Always test using the Dialogflow console to see if your intent is behaving as expected.

Now, let's set the default response of **user_order_id** intent to the following response from the bot:

*Order Status for Order ID: $order_id .The delivery guy is in your locality, your food will arrive in about 5 minutes.*

We are again using the parameter parsed from the **user_order_id** intent to prepare a reply to the user.

## User_Thanks Intent

Next, the user will possibly be thanking, if not something else, so we create a new intent called **user_thanks** to identify different ways the user is saying thank you. This is important because once the user says *thank you* in some way or another, our bot should reply the same.

We shouldn't just expect the user to say thanks after the delivery status default response and reply blindly but try to identify it using custom intents.

Figure 3-11 shows how our **user_thanks** intent looks.

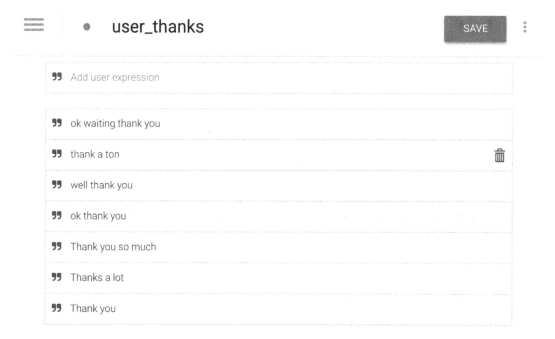

*Figure 3-11. Defining an intent when the user says thank you*

Now, it's time to say thank you to the user using the default response feature and mark this intent as the end of the conversation.

Let's add some text like, "*Thanks a lot for your cooperation,*" as our default response.

We can add more such responses so that the bot should look more realistic (see Figure 3-12).

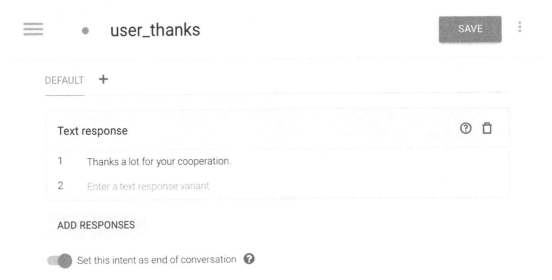

*Figure 3-12.  Adding a response against a user's intent in the agent*

Look at Figure 3-12 and see that we have enabled this intent as the end of conversation.

If we try to integrate our bot with Google Assistant, then enabling this means to close the microphone in Google Assistant when intent is finished.

Now at this point we have created our bot, built it as per our initial design and script, and trained it. Now, it's time to deploy it on web and see how it looks.

# Deploying Dialogflow Chatbot on the Web

In this part, we are going to integrate our bot with various platforms like Facebook Messenger, Twitter, Slack, etc., and see if they work. There are many more platforms where you can integrate this bot easily.

We will test our bot with Web Demo and Facebook Messenger for now.

Let's go to the Integrations page in our Dialogflow account and enable the **Web Demo.** You will be getting a pop-up like Figure 3-13. Click on the link in the pop-up.

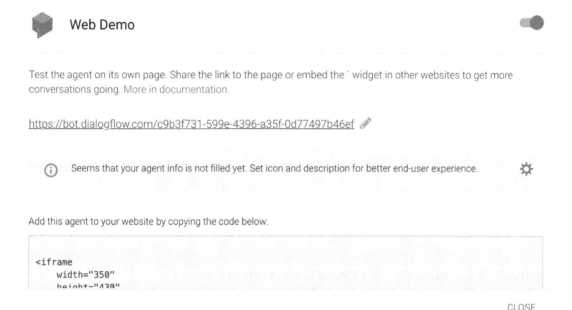

*Figure 3-13.* *Dialogflow's web demo link*

You will be seeing something similar to Figures 3-14.1 through 3-14.4. I tested my bot with the conversation we wrote, and my bot works like a charm.

***Figure 3-14.1.*** *OnlineEatsBot Demo Conversation Screen I*

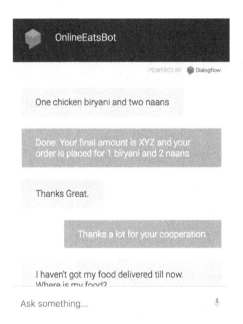

***Figure 3-14.2.*** *OnlineEatsBot Demo Conversation Screen II*

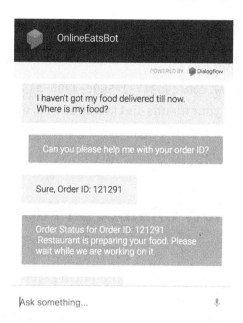

**Figure 3-14.3.**  *OnlineEatsBot Demo Conversation Screen III*

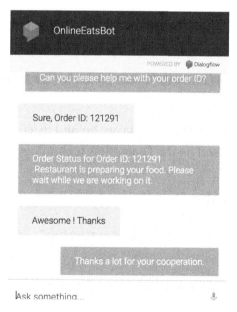

**Figure 3-14.4.**  *OnlineEatsBot Demo Conversation Screen IV*

Apart from this we can also embed this bot on our own website using the iframe code found in the pop-up window.

Talk to my **OnlineEatsBot** here:

`https://bot.dialogflow.com/c9b3f731-599e-4396-a35f-0d77497b46ef`

Share your own bot with your friends and family as well, and see the way they interact with the bot in a legitimate manner. If your chatbot is not doing something expected, then try to fix that.

# Integrate Dialogflow Chatbot on Facebook Messenger

In this section we'll try to integrate our same chatbot to Facebook Messenger so that our users on the Facebook platform can also use it without having to come to our website.

Let's go back to the integrations page in the Dialogflow dashboard and enable the Facebook Messenger icon, and then click on that, which should bring up a similar pop-up as before.

Here we need to go to Facebook, register an app, and get the required token.

- Verify Token (any string and is solely for your purposes)

- Page Access Token (Enter the token generated in the Facebook Developer Console)

The Dialogflow Facebook integration is very helpful to easily create a Facebook Messenger bot with NLU, based on the Dialogflow technology.

## Setting Up Facebook

To make our bot work the same way it worked in Facebook, we would need to do the following:

1. Create a Facebook account, if you haven't already.

2. Create Facebook page to which you can add your bot.

When a user visits your Facebook page and sends you a message, they'll be talking to your bot directly.

# Creating a Facebook App

The following are the steps to create an app:

1. Log into the Facebook Developer Console.

2. Click on **My Apps** in the upper right-hand corner.

3. Click on **Add a New App** and enter a name and contact e-mail address.

4. Click **Create App ID** as shown in the Figure 3-15 below.

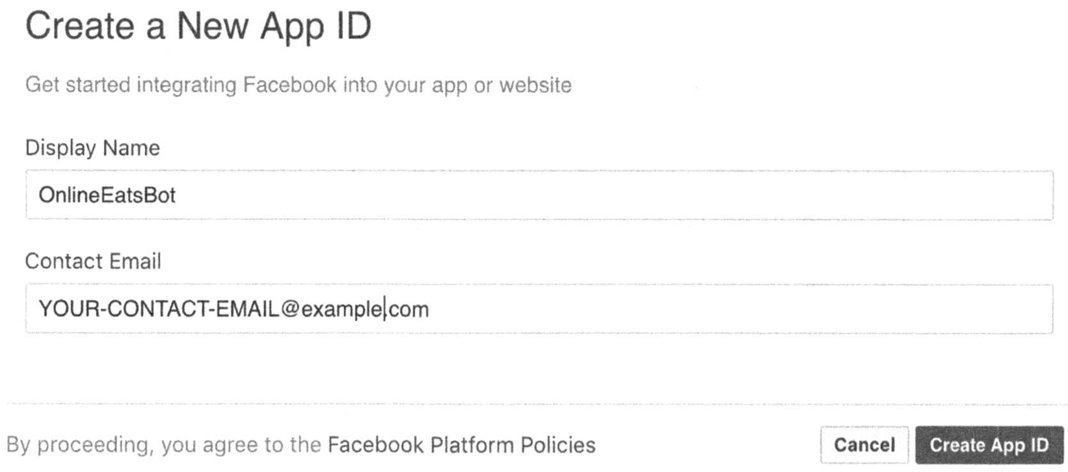

## Create a New App ID

Get started integrating Facebook into your app or website

Display Name

OnlineEatsBot

Contact Email

YOUR-CONTACT-EMAIL@example|com

By proceeding, you agree to the Facebook Platform Policies        Cancel     **Create App ID**

***Figure 3-15.*** *Creating a new app at Facebook Developer Platform*

5. On the next page, click the **Set Up** button for the **Messenger** option.

6. Under the **Token Generation** section, let's choose the Facebook page to which we want our bot to connect (see Figure 3-16).

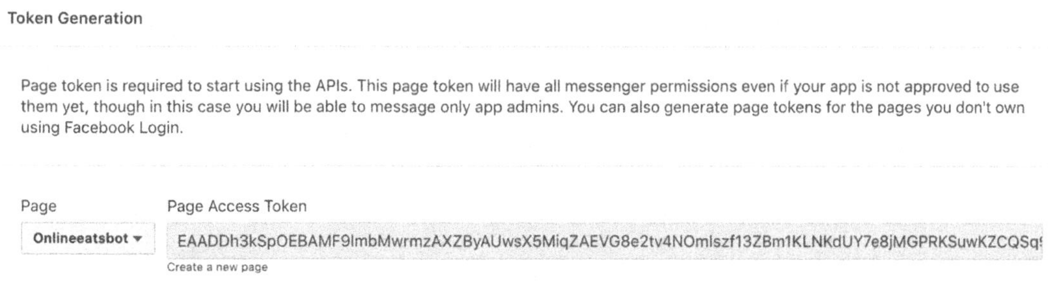

**Token Generation**

Page token is required to start using the APIs. This page token will have all messenger permissions even if your app is not approved to use them yet, though in this case you will be able to message only app admins. You can also generate page tokens for the pages you don't own using Facebook Login.

Page               Page Access Token

Onlineeatsbot ▾    EAADDh3kSpOEBAMF9lmbMwrmzAXZByAUwsX5MiqZAEVG8e2tv4NOmlszf13ZBm1KLNKdUY7e8jMGPRKSuwKZCQSq!
Create a new page

***Figure 3-16.*** *Generating token by selecting your Facebook page for your bot*

This will generate a **Page Access Token**. Keep this token handy, as we'll need to enter it in Dialogflow.

# Setting Up the Dialogflow Console

Here are the steps:

1. Click on the **Integrations** option in your Dialogflow console in the left menu and switch on **Facebook Messenger** if you haven't already. In the pop-up that opens, enter the following information as shown in the Figure 3-17 Setting up and integrating Dialogflow with Facebook Messenger:

   - **Verify Token:** this can be any string that you want and for your own purposes

   - **Page Access Token:** enter the token generated in the Facebook Developer Console

2. Click the **Start** button.

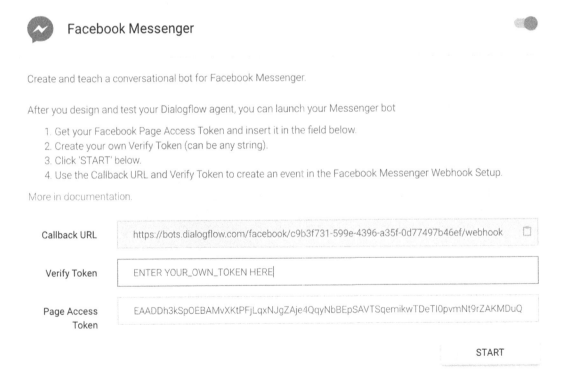

Facebook Messenger

Create and teach a conversational bot for Facebook Messenger.

After you design and test your Dialogflow agent, you can launch your Messenger bot

1. Get your Facebook Page Access Token and insert it in the field below.
2. Create your own Verify Token (can be any string).
3. Click 'START' below.
4. Use the Callback URL and Verify Token to create an event in the Facebook Messenger Webhook Setup.

More in documentation.

| Callback URL | https://bots.dialogflow.com/facebook/c9b3f731-599e-4396-a35f-0d77497b46ef/webhook |
|---|---|
| Verify Token | ENTER YOUR_OWN_TOKEN HERE |
| Page Access Token | EAADDh3kSpOEBAMvXKtPFjLqxNJgZAje4QqyNbBEpSAVTSqemikwTDeTI0pvmNt9rZAKMDuQ |

START

***Figure 3-17.*** *Setting up and integrating Dialogflow with Facebook Messenger*

You should get a message saying, "Bot was started." That means we are good to go.

You must be wondering what a callback URL, Verify Token, and Page Access Token are. Let's try to understand those.

## Callback URLs

A callback URL is nothing but a publicly accessible URL where Facebook will POST any real-time requests coming from your Facebook page.

Suppose you are trying to make payment for your food on **OnlineEats** and then you are redirected to a bank's payment page. Now, **OnlineEats** must be giving a callback URL to banks to which they can redirect the user after payment is done.

Here Facebook will not do any redirection but will take everything that our user messages in the page's chatbox and POST that to the webhook or callback URL.

Now, once we get the message on our server we do our intent classification and entities parsing and then formulate what you want to reply back to the user.

## Verify Token

A verify token is an arbitrary string sent to your endpoint when the subscription is verified. The reason why it's needed is to ensure that our server knows that the request is being made by Facebook and relates to the subscription we just configured.

Suppose somebody else gets to know your webhook and posts messages posing as Facebook, then *verify_token* will come into the picture, and you will verify if the source is correct or not. Based on this token you can handle POST requests from multiple sources as well because there will be different tokens defined for different sources but the same callback url.

## Access Tokens

Facebook APIs require Page Access Tokens to manage Facebook pages. They are unique to each page, admin, and app and have an expiration time.

---

**Note**   Keep the callback URL and Verify Token handy for configuring the webhook now.

---

# Configuring Webhooks

To configure our bot's webhook, let's go back to the Facebook Developer Console:

1.  Click the **Setup** button under the **Add a product** section for webhooks when you click on the dashboard. If you have not already subscribed to webhooks, then you will get an option saying "subscribe to this object." Click on this to get a new pop-up and enter the following information:

    -   **Callback URL**: this is the URL provided on the Facebook Messenger integration page.

    -   **Verify Token**: this is the Token you created.

2.  Go to Messenger ➤ Settings ➤ Setup Webhooks. You will get a pop-up like Figure 3-18. Add your callback url and verify the token.

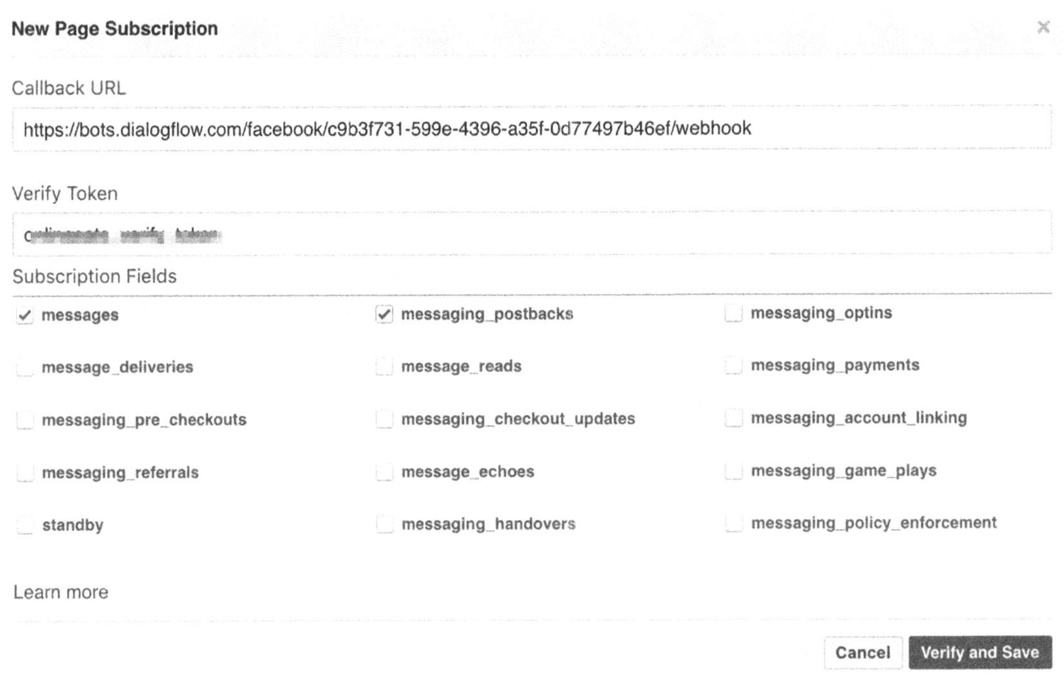

**New Page Subscription**                                                      ✕

Callback URL

https://bots.dialogflow.com/facebook/c9b3f731-599e-4396-a35f-0d77497b46ef/webhook

Verify Token

| ✓ messages | ✓ messaging_postbacks | messaging_optins |
| --- | --- | --- |
| message_deliveries | message_reads | messaging_payments |
| messaging_pre_checkouts | messaging_checkout_updates | messaging_account_linking |
| messaging_referrals | message_echoes | messaging_game_plays |
| standby | messaging_handovers | messaging_policy_enforcement |

Subscription Fields

Learn more

Cancel    Verify and Save

*Figure 3-18.*  *Setting up webhooks in Facebook for Dialogflow bot*

3. Check the **messages** and **messaging_postbacks** options under **Subscription Fields.** You can definitely choose whichever is needed for your use-case.

4. Click the **Verify and Save** button. Check Figure 3-18 for reference.

You'll be taken back to the settings page and **Webhooks** should have a "Complete" status. Make sure to select a page to which you can subscribe your webhook for page events.

## Testing the Messenger Bot

To be able to make our bot available for testing, we'll need to make our app public:

1. Click on **App Review** in the left menu of the Facebook Developer Console.

2. Click on the switch under **Make <Your APP Name> public?** If you get an **Invalid Privacy Policy URL** prompt, then go to the Basic Settings link in the dialog box and, if you haven't already, put any URL for the Privacy Policy URL, for the time being and then click on Save Changes. Now, go back to the **App Review** page and try to switch the app to public again.

3. You'll be prompted to choose a category for your app.

4. Choose **Education** from the list. Feel free to choose whichever suits your bot best.

5. Click the **Confirm** button as shown in the Figure 3-19, Making your facebook app public.

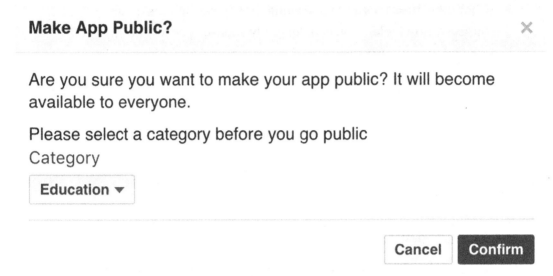

*Figure 3-19.* *Making your facebook app public*

We will also need to create a username for our page. This is the username users will chat with when using our bot. To set the username, click the **Create Page @Username** link under the About section of your page, as shown in Figure 3-20. This is helpful to share your page or bot with people using just a short name.

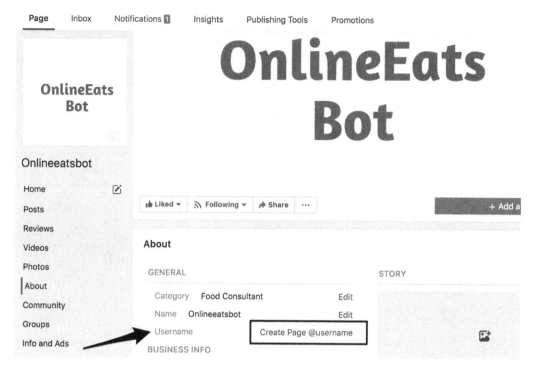

***Figure 3-20.***  *Creating your Facebook bot's page username*

Let's test the same flow of our bot on Facebook Messenger that we tested on Dialogflow's website. You should be able to see how my Facebook Messenger bot responded by referring from Figure 3-21.1 up-to Figure 3-21.4.

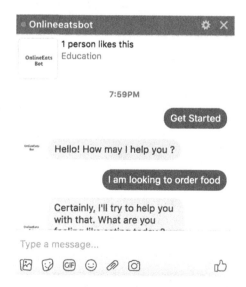

***Figure 3-21.1.***  *Facebook Messenger OnlineEatsBot Demo Screen I*

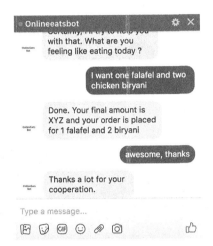

*Figure 3-21.2.* *Facebook Messenger OnlineEatsBot Demo Screen II*

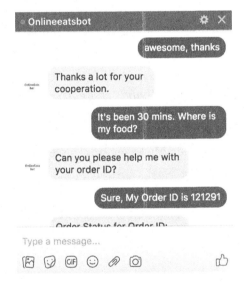

*Figure 3-21.3.* *Facebook Messenger OnlineEatsBot Demo Screen III*

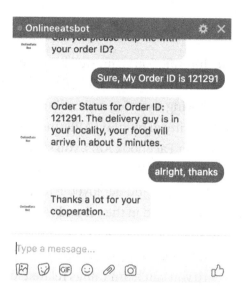

***Figure 3-21.4.*** *Facebook Messenger OnlineEatsBot Demo Screen IV*

And that, folks, is how we build our bot.

Chapter 4 is going be even more interesting. In Chapter 4, we will try to achieve the same without having to depend on Dialogflow's API or dashboard.

It's always good when you have full control over everything you have, isn't it?

Note: You can go to your account settings and export an agent or import other agents directly. You can download the zip file (**OnlineEatsBot.zip**). You can use this zip to import this into Dialogflow and play with the chatbot we built in this chapter.

You must be wondering, what if I wanted to make the order placement in real-time and find the order status using APIs of the vendor/restaurant and reply to the user accordingly? It could be any API call you want to make—retrieve the data in real-time and formulate the bot's response. It's time to know how to do that before we wrap up this chapter and get ready for the next one.

Let's learn about something called "**Fulfillment**" in Dialogflow.

# Fulfillment

In order to get some real-time information requested by a user, we need to develop some API or use existing ones. To achieve that using Dialogflow, we would need to set up fulfillment, which requires deploying a service and calling an API.

We will not go into the nitty-gritty of building APIs and how to deploy it but if you have ever tried using any Google or Facebook APIs, you should be familiar with at least how to call them.

I have built a small Flask-based API and deployed it to Heroku. I will be using it for fulfillment, which just takes any order_id in the url and returns a random order_status. If you are not familiar with Heroku, then do not worry, you can run the code provided on your local system and test it. In the upcoming chapter, we'll be deploying lots of application using Heroku where you can learn things related to it.

In the code you can read how order_identity, intentName, etc., are parsed.

Find the code here: **flask_onlineeats_demo.zip**

Request URL: `https://radiant-bayou-76095.herokuapp.com/onlineeatsbot/ api/v1.0/order_status/`

So, in Dialogflow Fulfillment will POST the JSON response from the intent to this URL, which you would need to parse to get the relevant entities and their values and do specific actions.

You can also try to deploy the sample Flask App code on Heroku and have your own endpoint working in your bot for fulfillment.

Now, Dialogflow will POST the JSON response of the intent for which the webhook call is enabled on our endpoint. It has the code to parse the **order_id** entity and take actions based on that. Currently, the code only returns a randomly chosen status from a list.

To test if the API is working, go to POSTMAN and test it using the sample data in Figure 3-22. If you are running the Flask app on local, then use the local url.

***Figure 3-22.*** *Testing the fulfillment API deployed on heroku in POSTMAN*

# Enabling Webhook

So, let's go to the fulfillment page in Dialogflow and try to enable webhook
(see Figure 3-23).

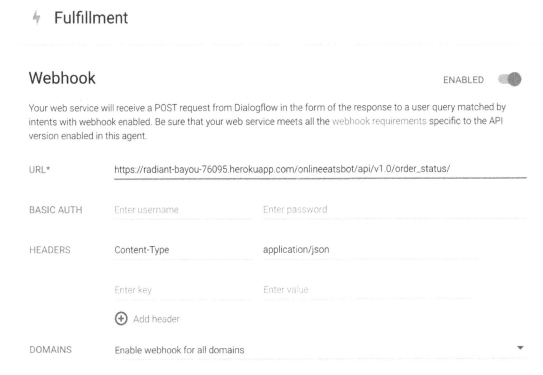

**Figure 3-23.**  Setting up webhook for fulfillment in Dialogflow

Make sure you have enabled webhook call for **user_order_id** intent (see Figure 3-24).

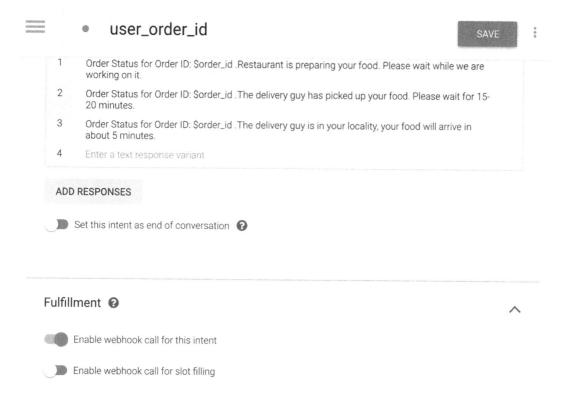

*Figure 3-24.*  *Enabling webhook call for specific intent*

Dialogflow will POST a JSON body to your webhook URL, which will look like Figure 3-25.

## JSON

```json
1   {
2     "responseId": "6e48703b-0259-4d6c-81a1-c6e6b2da0d07",
3     "queryResult": {
4       "queryText": "Order ID is 234",
5       "parameters": {
6         "order_id": 234
7       },
8       "allRequiredParamsPresent": true,
9       "fulfillmentText": "Order ID: 234.0. Restaurant preparing the food",
10      "fulfillmentMessages": [
11        {
12          "text": {
13            "text": [
14              "Order ID: 234.0. Restaurant preparing the food"
15            ]
16          }
17        }
18      ],
19      "webhookPayload": {
20        "facebook": {
21          "text": "Order ID: 234.0. Restaurant preparing the food"
22        }
23      },
24      "intent": {
25        "name": "projects/hellooa-fdfca/agent/intents/9a39f983-74e8-487c-bb67
              -a22b728fc3d2",
26        "displayName": "user_order_id"
27      },
28      "intentDetectionConfidence": 0.97,
29      "diagnosticInfo": {
30        "webhook_latency_ms": 200
31      },
32      "languageCode": "en"
33    },
34    "webhookStatus": {
35      "message": "Webhook execution successful"
36    }
37  }
```

CLOSE          COPY

***Figure 3-25.*** *Incoming JSON data from Dialogflow to our webhook endpoint*

# Checking the Response

Dialogflow expects a response from your web service in the format shown in Figure 3-26 whenever they POST an intent's JSON response (shown in Figure 3-25) to your web service.

```
1  {
2  "fulfillmentText": "This is a text response",
3  "fulfillmentMessages": [
4      {
5        "card": {
6          "title": "card title",
7          "subtitle": "card text",
8          "imageUri": "https://assistant.google.com/static/images/molecule/Molecule-Formation-stop.png",
9          "buttons": [
10           {
11             "text": "button text",
12             "postback": "https://assistant.google.com/"
13           }
14         ]
15       }
16     }
17  ],
18  "source": "example.com",
19  "payload": {
20     "google": {
21       "expectUserResponse": true,
22       "richResponse": {
23         "items": [
24           {
25             "simpleResponse": {
26               "textToSpeech": "this is a simple response"
27             }
28           }
29         ]
30       }
31     },
32     "facebook": {
33       "text": "Hello, Facebook!"
34     },
35     "slack": {
36       "text": "This is a text response for Slack."
37     }
38  },
39  "outputContexts": [
40     {
41       "name": "projects/${PROJECT_ID}/agent/sessions/${SESSION_ID}/contexts/context name",
42       "lifespanCount": 5,
43       "parameters": {
44         "param": "param value"
45       }
46     }
47  ],
48  "followupEventInput": {
49     "name": "event name",
50     "languageCode": "en-US",
51     "parameters": {
52       "param": "param value"
53  }}}
54
55
```

**Figure 3-26.** *Response from the webhook URL expected by Dialogflow*

If you are thinking that your API's response should be exactly in the same format as Figure 3-26, then relax—that's not the case. Your intent won't throw errors because all of the keys in the JSON body are optional.

Here is how my API response looks and works perfectly:

```
{
    "fulfillmentText": "Order ID: 9999. It's on the way",
    "payload": {
        "facebook": {
            "text": "Order ID: 9999. It's on the way"
        }
    }
}
```

When I try to hit the same API again I get a different order status text but with the same format expected by Dialogflow engine.

```
{
    "fulfillmentText": "Order ID: 9999. Rider has picked up your food,
    please wait for another 10-15 minutes",
    "payload": {
        "facebook": {
            "text": "Order ID: 9999. Rider has picked up your food, please
            wait for another 10-15 minutes"
        }
    }
}
```

**fulfillmentText** is the key that matters for the agent to reply something back to the user.

Now, try the bot with the public URL or in the Dialogflow agent itself to see the responses coming from the API instead of the default static responses we added earlier.

This is how we can integrate an external API or our own API using Dialogflow's fulfillment feature into our chatbot to make things dynamic and real-time.

# Summary

In this chapter we learned about Dialogflow and how to use Dialogflow to build a chatbot. We learned to define intents and their respective entities. We built a simple food ordering chatbot that understands the order food intent from the user and also understands what food items the user has asked for as well as the quantity. We also enhanced our chatbot to let users ask about the status of their order and take their order ID from them and formulate a response with different order statuses.

We also learned about fulfillment in Dialogflow, where we pulled the status of the order from our own API and gave the response to the user based on that. We learned to create a web demo of our chatbot, and we also integrated our bot with Messenger. At this point, you should have a fair idea of how a chatbot works end-to-end.

In the next chapter we are going to try the harder way of building chatbots. Yes, you heard it right. We are going to remove the dependency from tools like Dialogflow and build everything ourselves programmatically. Let's get ready for the next chapter, because that is going to be even more fun when you have built everything from scratch yourself. It's like training and taming your own chatbots.

See you in the next chapter.

# CHAPTER 4

# Building Chatbots the Hard Way

"Building Chatbots the Hard Way" is not too hard to learn. It's the hard way of building chatbots to have full control over your own chatbots. If you want to build everything yourself, then you take the hard route. The harder route is hard when you go through it but beautiful and clear when you look back.

*It is a rough road that leads to the heights of greatness.*

—Lucius Annaeus Seneca

If you know Python well and have a bit of understanding on how to setup packages, etc., you won't have any issues learning this chapter. If you are a developer, it should be easy for you. If you are a manager or non-technical person, you can still do the steps one-by-one as mentioned in each section and get things done. I strongly recommend everyone complete this chapter so that you learn core things about building chatbots.

This chapter not only teaches you to build chatbots from scratch but also shows you how core machine learning (ML) works with NLP with the help of Rasa NLU. As mentioned in the first chapter on this book, it is always good to have decision trees when you are building chatbots. In this chapter, we'll barely be using any rules, but ML is not at that stage yet to be 100 percent reliable. So, this decision is based completely on your use-case and whether you want to apply some business logic along with your ML models or not. Sometimes, your ML model may work so well that you don't need any heuristics at all. But in my experience, when you go on to sell your chatbots or commercialize them, you have to be a little careful. No functionality is better than having a functionality that doesn't make sense.

© Sumit Raj 2019
S. Raj, *Building Chatbots with Python*, https://doi.org/10.1007/978-1-4842-4096-0_4

We'll be using an open-source library called Rasa NLU for learning how to build chatbots from scratch without using any cloud services like Dialogflow, Watson, wit.ai, etc. Remember Rasa NLU is a very sophisticated library and has lots of features in it. We are only going to touch upon the concepts and features that are important for us to build our chatbot.

# What Is Rasa NLU?

Rasa NLU is an open-source NLP library for intent classification and entity extraction in chatbots. It helps you build and write custom NLP for your chatbots.

There are two parts of Rasa that we'll be covering in this chapter.

- **Rasa NLU:** With Rasa NLU we'll be learning to prepare our training data for our chatbot, writing configuration files, choosing a pipeline and training the model. Lastly, we will be predicting the intent of a text using our model. We'll also be learning how to parse entities using Rasa NLU.

- **Rasa Core:** In the second part we'll be learning to train the **Rasa Core** dialog management model to prepare responses back to the user. This section becomes very important when you have a variety of intents in your chatbot and their follow-up questions or responses. Instead of writing lots of conditions in our decision tree and spending hours debugging it in case of a big enterprise-level application, it's better to teach the model to create responses. It'll be interesting to see how well our trained model performs in doing that. We can't just spit out anything to the user in the form of text; it should make sense.

# Why Should I Use Rasa NLU?

Rasa NLU is not just any other library with a bunch of methods to do some things. It has the capability of building almost any kind of chatbot that you can imagine. Rasa brings you the magical capability of training the machine to understand the meaning of a text rather than you writing rules to understand it.

Let's look at the following points on why we should use Rasa NLU:

- Rasa NLU is an actively maintained project and has a good community to support it.

- If we don't want to share our user's sensitive data with a third party, we must use open-source tools like Rasa NLU to build chatbots from scratch. This way all the data remains and gets processed on our own servers.

- Depending on third-party services for training your data and finding the intents of user utterances will require you to call APIs that may not always be reliable. What happens to your chatbot application if their server is down?

- Using Rasa NLU for building chatbots will give you full command over your chatbots. You can train, tune, and optimize it the way you want with the data you want. With Rasa NLU we can experiment with which ML algorithm works best for our dataset rather than depending on a fixed algorithm.

# Diving Straight Into Rasa NLU

In this section we'll dive straight into the hands-on part and try installing the Rasa stack and start working on building our ML models by training our data. We'll be using some of the cooler open-source libraries to make our lives easier.

## Installing Rasa

To install Rasa, run the following pip command that we tried in previous chapters for installing spaCy. Note that we'll be using Rasa version 0.13.2.

```
pip install rasa-nlu==0.13.2
```

Rasa NLU has multiple components for classifying intents and recognizing entities. Different components of Rasa have their own sets of dependencies.

When we train our model, Rasa NLU checks that all the required dependencies are installed. If you want to install the full requirements needed to entirely use the Rasa library, you can execute the following steps:

```
git clone https://github.com/RasaHQ/rasa_nlu.git #Clone the repo
cd rasa_nlu #Get into the rasa directory
pip install -r alt_requirements/requirements_full.txt #Install full
requirements
```

The first step may take some time. Be as patient as earth until it completes.

## Deciding a Pipeline in Rasa

Pipeline is nothing but a set of algorithms to be used to train your model. Rasa NLU has two widely used pipelines called `spacy_sklearn` and `tensorflow_embedding`. Let's learn a bit about both.

`spacy_sklearn`

- *spacy_sklearn* pipeline makes use of pre-trained word vectors from either GloVe algorithm or an algorithm developed by the Facebook AI team called fastText.

- *spacy_sklearn* works amazingly well in situations where, suppose you have an utterance like, "What is the weather in Boston?" When we train our model on the same utterance example and then ask it to predict the intent for, "What is the weather in London?" our model is now intelligent enough to know that both the words "Boston" and "London" are similar, and they belong to the same intent.

- This pipeline is very useful with small sets of data.

  `tensorflow_embedding`

- *tensorflow_embedding* pipeline doesn't make use of any pre-trained word vectors like spacy_sklearn, but it adjusts itself as per our own provided dataset.

- The good thing about *tensorflow_embedding* pipeline is that our word vectors will be as per our domain.

- To explain how *tensorflow_embedding* works with an example, in English language, the word "play" may be closely related to "a sport" or "an activity of enjoyment or recreation," and it may seem it very different from the words "an act." In a theater domain, "play" and "an act" are closely related, where "play" means "a form of literature written by a playwright," and it is very necessary to tell our model to learn specific to our domain and not get confused due to some pre-trained model.

# Training and Building a Chatbot From Scratch

If you have gone through Chapter 3 of this book, you must be familiar with the "Food Ordering Chatbot" we built using Dialogflow. You must be aware of intents, entities, and responses back to the end user by a chatbot.

Similarly, we are going to take a use-case of a chatbot and build it from scratch in this chapter. You need not necessarily use the same example. Feel free to find a use-case of your own, follow the steps in this chapter, and build your own chatbot at the completion of this chapter.

We are going to build a horoscope bot that understands user queries and tells them their horoscope for the day. So, let's get started.

## Building a Horoscope Bot

In this example of building a chatbot completely on our own using the open-source library Rasa NLU, we are going to build a Horoscope Bot. Let's decide the scope of this chatbot and see what it does and can do.

- The Horoscope Bot should be able to understand greetings and reply with a greeting.

- The bot should be able to understand if the user is asking for a horoscope.

- The bot should be able to ask the horoscope sign of the user if the user doesn't provide it.

- If the user doesn't know his/her horoscope sign, the bot should ask the user's date of birth (DOB) and find it for them.

- The bot should subscribe/unsubscribe the user to get the daily horoscope.

- The bot should learn from existing responses to formulate a new response.

- The bot should be able to handle spelling mistakes by the user.

It is pretty simple what our bot is supposed to do here.

Possible intents

- Greeting Intent: User starting with a greeting

- Get Horoscope Intent: User asking for horoscope

- User's Horoscope Intent: User telling the horoscope sign

- User's DOB Intent: User telling his/her DOB

- Subscription Intent: User asking for subscription

Depending on the way you design your bot and write code, you may or may not need all of the above intents or you may need to define some extra intents as well to cover all the use-cases we want our bot to do. As we move forward in this chapter, we'll try to build the bot that does the basic task of giving a horoscope; later as a part of the exercise, we can add more use-cases to it.

Well, this is pretty much what we have been doing so far to recognize the possible intents based on a simple possible conversation between a bot and a user.

# Conversation Script Between the Horoscope Bot and the User

Let's create a possible conversation script between our chatbot and the user. As mentioned in the first chapter, writing a conversation script is like preparing a software requirement document before building the software. It may change later but gives you an overall view of what's going to happen in the final chatbot application.

The following is what our conversation between the user and the bot looks like:

**User:** Hello

**Horoscope Bot:** Hello! Hope you are doing well.

**User:** I want to know my horoscope.

**Horoscope Bot:** Sure, may I know your horoscope sign?

**User:** Capricorm

**Horoscope Bot:** Sorry, did you mean Capricorn?

**User:** Yes.

**Horoscope Bot:** Alright, Here is your horoscope for today. Chances are that you'll feel upbeat and positive today. Share this energy with others who feel less than content. Your attitude can have a profound effect on friends, partners, spouse, and children. Neighbors and extended family can pick up on your spirit without you even realizing it. If someone is hurt or angry, be encouraging. Everything will eventually work out.

**Horoscope Bot:** Would you like to subscribe for the daily updates? If yes, just say subscribe.

**User:** Yes, please subscribe.

**Horoscope Bot:** Great, you are subscribed now. Have a good day.

This conversation is just to have a fair idea of how our chatbot conversation is going to look. We may or may not want to change the flow of the conversation based on our needs.

We can have our chatbot model itself trained to prepare a valid response instead of writing a bunch of if...else statements.

# Preparing Data for Chatbot

Rasa NLU has multiple ways of defining the intents and their entities on our custom data. It supports data in markdown, in JSON as a single file, or as a directory containing multiple files.

We are going to discuss the most difficult, but highly scalable, method first. Creating JSON files is difficult by hand but programmatically very easy and scalable.

# Creating Data for Model in JSON Format

The JSON format of the data that Rasa NLU expects has a top-level object called *rasa_nlu_data*, with the keys *common_examples*, *entity_synonyms*, and *regex_features*.

The most important one with which we are going to be working is *common_examples*. The following is the skeleton form of how our JSON data is going to look:

```
{
    "rasa_nlu_data": {
        "common_examples": [],
        "regex_features" : [],
        "entity_synonyms": []
    }
}
```

The *common_examples* key in our JSON data is the central place that'll be used to train our model. We will be adding all our training examples in the *common_examples* array.

*regex_features* is a tool to help the intent classifier recognize entities or intents and improve the accuracy of intent classification.

Let's start writing our JSON file. Let's call it **data.json.**

1. Create a folder called **horoscope_bot**.

2. Change the current working directory to horoscope_bot.

3. Start Jupyter Notebook #jupyter notebook.

4. Create a new folder called **data**.

5. Click on the data folder and go to "Text File" under New menu in Jupyter Notebook.

6. Click on the name of the file created and change the name to **data.json** and write your intents for your chatbots.

For Steps 5 and 6, feel free to use your favorite editors like Sublime, Notepad++, PyCharm, etc., to work with the JSON file.

This following is what my **data.json** under **data** folder looks like:

```json
{
  "rasa_nlu_data": {
    "common_examples": [
      {
        "text": "Hello",
        "intent": "greeting",
        "entities": []
      },
      {
        "text": "I want to know my Horoscope",
        "intent": "get_horoscope",
        "entities": []
      },
      {
        "text": "Can you please tell me my horoscope?",
        "intent": "get_horoscope",
        "entities": []
      },
      {
        "text": "Please subscribe me",
        "intent": "subscription"
      }
    ],
    "regex_features": [],
    "entity_synonyms": []
  }
}
```

Well as you can see, it looks very clumsy to prepare this by hand. You must be remembering the nice and easy method we had in Dialogflow. So, let's check a cool and interesting tool for creating training data in the format that Rasa expects. It was created by Polgár András, and it's also pretty much good for inspecting and modifying existing data that we prepared earlier. This tool saves a lot of time if you are working on a small project where you have to create the data by hand. It's always a good idea to visualize the data in any application you are building that is completely data-driven.

So, just save the earlier **data.json** file we created until we extend the data collection using a better method.

## Visualizing and Modifying Rasa's JSON Data Format

In this section we'll make use of a tool called Rasa NLU trainer to visualize our data. (i.e., the data that we have created so far). This tool helps us in annotating the data as well. If you remember when the Dialogflow interface was explained in Chapter 3, it was so easy to define entities, their names, and the types. We are going to do the same using an open-source tool.

Rasa NLU trainer is a very nice and handy tool to edit our training data right from our browser itself. Handling JSON data is tricky and also can lead to errors. With this handy tool we can easily add more examples to our training data or edit the existing ones. It saves a lot of time from manually annotating the data. rasa-nlu-trainer is a javascript-based tool, so we would need to install node.js to run this tool on our system. It doesn't take more than 5 minutes to do that. Let's get this set up by following these steps:

1. Go to `https://www.npmjs.com/get-npm` and download node.js.

2. Install the package on your system as guided on the website. Once installed, go to a fresh terminal/command line interface on your system and type "npm" to see if it works.

I have installed LTS version 8.11.4. Once installed, run the following command to install rasa-nlu-trainer:

```
sudo npm i -g rasa-nlu-trainer
```

After the successful installation this command, you'll see logs similar to the following:

```
[fsevents] Success: "/usr/local/lib/node_modules/rasa-nlu-trainer/
node_modules/fsevents/lib/binding/Release/node-v57-darwin-x64/fse.node"
already installed
Pass --update-binary to reinstall or --build-from-source to recompile
npm WARN slick-carousel@1.8.1 requires a peer of jquery@>=1.8.0 but none is
installed. You must install peer dependencies yourself.

+ rasa-nlu-trainer@0.2.7
added 492 packages in 10.14s
```

Even if your message doesn't look like this, as long as it doesn't throw any errors then don't worry. We'll get to know in a moment if our rasa-nlu-trainer is successfully installed and works well.

Let's go to our data folder that we created earlier in our terminal and run the following command:

```
rasa-nlu-trainer
```

Typing this command will crank up a local server on port 55703 and open it in the default browser. It will look something like Figure 4-1.

*Figure 4-1.* *rasa-nlu-trainer in localhost*

As you can see, all of our existing data from data.json is picked by this amazing tool for us to delete or edit and we can also add new examples from here and it will keep on extending the data.json file.

I would suggest that you add more data to your intents for better training of the model. You can get this data.json in the source code zip or repo provided by the publisher, if you are trying to build the same chatbot explained in this chapter.

Just as we selected the entities within utterances to define them in Chapter 3 using Dialogflow, we can do the same using this tool and give names to our entities for parsing later. So, click on the toggle button of the example, select the text, and add an entity by giving it a name.

I have added five to six utterance examples in each of the intents I have defined. The more examples we add, the better it is for the model to be trained and provide better accuracy.

If you look at the data.json file now, it will have more examples automatically added to it. So, go ahead and verify your data.json file to see if you have all your added examples from **rasa-nlu-trainer** UI.

You'll also notice in the data.json file that the entities you might have defined using the rasa-nlu-trainer UI are captured in the ***common_examples*** list as having **start** and **end** keys, which tells the model at what point the particular entity value starts in the example and when it ends.

The same dictionary object also depicts the value of the entity and the name of the entity we defined. For our example, it looks like the following:

```
{
        "text": "19-01",
        "intent": "dob_intent",
        "entities": [
          {
            "start": 0,
            "end": 2,
            "value": "19",
            "entity": "DD"
          },
          {
            "start": 3,
            "end": 5,
            "value": "01",
            "entity": "MM"
          }
        ]
      }
```

# Training the Chatbot Model

In this section we are going to train a model on the data we prepared. As we used Jupyter Notebook for our file creation and management, we will be creating a new .ipynb and start writing our Python code to train our model by choosing one of the pipelines we discussed earlier in this chapter.

# Creating a Configuration File

Let's create a JSON file again in the same way we created one earlier using Jupyter and name it **config.json**. Let's keep it outside our data folder (i.e., in the horoscope_bot that is our project directory).

Add the following configuration to it:

```
{
  "pipeline":"tensorflow_embedding",
  "path":"./models/nlu",
  "data":"./data/data.json"
}
```

As you can see, there are some important configuration parameters done in our config.json file. Let's try to understand them.

- **pipeline**: Pipeline is going to specify what featurizers or feature extractors are going to be used to crunch text messages and extract necessary information. In our case, we are using *tensorflow_embedding*.

- **path**: path is essentially the directory where we keep our model after the training. We are going to keep our model in the /models/nlu folder.

- **data**: data is the path we need to specify; it's basically where our training data sits.

As we are done with our config.json file, let's move on to some Python code to train our ML model.

---

## YAML CONFIGURATION

You can also use .yml file as config files like below. You can get the example config.yml files in github repo.

- **Example 1:**

  ```
  language: "en"
  pipeline: "tensorflow_embedding"
  ```

- **Example 2:**

```
language: "en"
    pipeline:
    - name: "nlp_spacy"
    - name: "tokenizer_spacy"
    - name: "intent_entity_featurizer_regex"
    - name: "intent_featurizer_spacy"
    - name: "ner_crf"
    - name: "ner_synonyms"
    - name: "intent_classifier_sklearn"
```

All incoming messages are processed as per the sequence of components defined. The defined components are run in a sequential manner, one by one, and hence are called the processing pipeline. Different components are used for different purposes, such as entity extraction, intent classification, pre-processing, etc.

The benefit of such a format is that we can specify the predefined pipelines by Rasa in a clear manner.

# Writing Python Code to Train the Model and Predict

Let's open up a new .ipynb file and start writing our code. Let's name the ipynb as rasa-nlu.ipynb. Make sure you have already successfully installed rasa-nlu==0.13.2 for the Python version you are using.

The following is what our code looks like to use our data.json and config.json in Python and train a model using *tensorflow_embedding* pipeline.

```python
from rasa_nlu.training_data import load_data
from rasa_nlu.model import Trainer
from rasa_nlu import config
from rasa_nlu.model import Interpreter

def train_horoscopebot(data_json, config_file, model_dir):
    training_data = load_data(data_json)
    trainer = Trainer(config.load(config_file))
    trainer.train(training_data)
    model_directory = trainer.persist(model_dir, fixed_model_name =
    'horoscopebot')
```

```
def predict_intent(text):
    interpreter = Interpreter.load('./models/nlu/default/horoscopebot')
    print(interpreter.parse(text))
```

In the first section of the code, we import all the necessary libraries needed from rasa_nlu package. Then we define two methods called *train_horoscopebot* and *predict_intent*, where the first method trains the model given the data, config_file, and model_directory (place to store the models) and predict_intent method uses the **Interpreter** model from rasa_nlu to load the pre-trained model files and gives the user the ability to predict any new text examples.

## Training the Model

We run the below snippet to call our train_horoscopebot method with the respective parameters

```
train_horoscopebot('./data/data.json', 'config.json', './models/nlu')
```

After running this code in our rasa-nlu.ipynb, we will get an output like this:

```
Epochs: 100%|████████████████████████| 300/300 [00:01<00:00, 175.69it/s,
loss=0.075, acc=1.000]
```

The code for training the chatbot model will create the models folder, which you can see using Jupyter or using your file explorer or finder app. It will create a bunch of index, meta, and pickle files at the model directory destination we provided.

## Predicting From the Model

Let's call the predict_intent method by passing a text to see how our trained model performs.

```
predict_intent("I am looking for my horoscope for today. I am wondering if
you can tell me that.")
```

The method itself prints the output. For the above text, my output looks like the following:

```
INFO:tensorflow:Restoring parameters from ./models/nlu/default/
horoscopebot/intent_classifier_tensorflow_embedding.ckpt

{
  "intent": {
    "name": "get_horoscope",
    "confidence": 0.9636583924293518
  },
  "entities": [],
  "intent_ranking": [
    {
      "name": "get_horoscope",
      "confidence": 0.9636583924293518
    },
    {
      "name": "dob_intent",
      "confidence": 0.03462183475494385
    },
    {
      "name": "greeting",
      "confidence": 0
    },
    {
      "name": "subscription",
      "confidence": 0
    }
  ],
  "text": "I am looking for my horoscope for today. I am wondering if you
  can tell me that."
}
```

Wow! Isn't it magical? Our model has predicted this text with a confidence of 96 percent. You can see in the provided ipynb file that our model does well in predicting other intents as well. This is the power of tensorflow and ML overall. Needless to say, rasa_nlu library makes it so easy to believe. So, it's time for you go back in retrospection, and if you remember Chapter 3 of this book, then you must remember whenever we used to add a new example, the Dialogflow used to re-train the model. It was actually doing the same as we just did, behind the scenes. We couldn't have changed the model or tuned any parameter there, but we can do that all now with full control.

Now that we have successfully built and trained a model using tensorflow and tested it as well, we'll move on to the next topic of Dialog Management. I would request you test all the scenarios your bot might be facing so that you know the points where your model is not performing well and, accordingly, you can add more data or tune the parameters if needed.

Also, remember that you only need to re-train the model whenever there is a change in the training data. If there is no change in the training data, we can load the existing training model to keep predicting on new examples.

# Dialog Management Using Rasa Core

In this section we are going to get our hands dirty by training another model for Rasa Core dialog management. Remember, at this point we have a model ready to predict the intent of the text, we can write some Python code to formulate responses, and we can reply back to the customer. But what if we want to add more intents to our bot? Is that scalable in the case of a bigger application with lots of features? The answer is no. Here dialog management from Rasa Core comes to the rescue.

If you have ever tried to use any bot on any platform, you must have seen it failing in certain conditions. Yes, we all have been there and it still exists as today's bot fails to manage the contexts of the conversation miserably or follow the suit of conversation. With the help of Rasa Core's ML-based dialog framework we can fix this issue easily. Rasa Core is well-proven for enterprise-level applications and used by thousands of developers because it is production-ready, easy to use and extend, and, most importantly, open source.

# Understanding More on Rasa Core and Dialog System

Before we actually move to the coding part of Rasa Core for our dialog management model, it's really important to understand why and where this is coming from.

We'll try to understand how we have been doing things so far for building the chatbots and how this is going to be changed forever.

Let's take an example:

If we were to build a simple chatbot that would help users book flight/bus/movie/train tickets, the easiest way would be to create a state machine or decision trees, write a bunch of if...else, and it would be done. This would work but wouldn't scale. If a customer is having a good experience initially with something, they want to use it more. By some heuristics, we can show a chatbot to be intelligent but not for very long. When the control flow of the code goes from try block to except block, we start scratching our heads.

Figure 4-2 is a simple representation of how a state machine for building this chatbot may look.

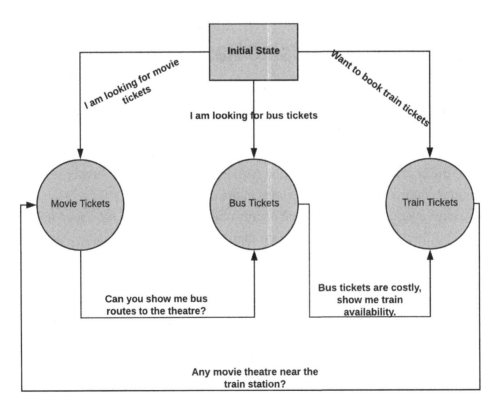

***Figure 4-2.*** *State diagram representation for ticket booking chatbot*

If we look at our state diagram, it may work for a normal conversation where the user is looking for movie, bus, or train tickets or wants to book a bus ticket after asking for movie tickets. What if the user asks for both bus and movie tickets together? You may say that we can add a couple more if…else statements in our already nested code to handle that. If you are a good developer, it won't take you much time to write an in-out from a state machine or extend your decision tree. But think of the situation when these conditions start growing exponentially and you have to keep adding cases to handle that and they start interfering with each other as well.

Our brain works in a way where we learn and relearn. If a kid doesn't know what a fire is going to do to them, they touch it, but when it hurts them, they do not do it again. They reinforce a fact that it's harmful. It works similarly in the case of rewards— when you do something and get something, you associate a fact that doing something brings rewards or better rewards and then you intend to do that again. This is called reinforcement learning in ML, where a machine learns how to behave in a particular situation by performing actions and understanding the results. Reinforcement learning is sometimes not the best approach, such as in situations where data is not sufficient to be learned, data quality is not good to learn the reward scenarios, etc.

Figure 4-3 is a diagram to help you understand how Rasa Core fits well within the Rasa Stack and its role along with Rasa NLU, which we have been learning so far.

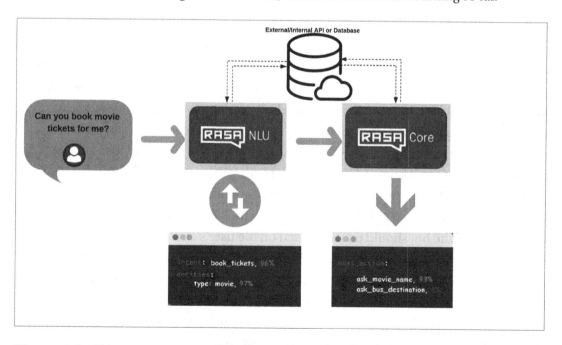

***Figure 4-3.*** *Diagram representing the working of Rasa NLU and Rasa Core*

With Rasa Core, we can specify all of the things our bot is supposed to say or do. These are called *actions*. One action might be to say a greeting to the user or to query a database, or it could be to retrieve some information using some web service or API.

Rasa Core provides the facility to train our probabilistic model to predict what action has to be taken based on the historical conversation of the user or users. Imagine doing it without an ML model and writing hundreds of use-cases to figure out what response or action should be sent or executed. In simple terms, Rasa Core solves this problem for you.

Let's look at the side-by-side user vs. bot conversation that we built in Chapter 3 while building an OnlineEatsBot.

| User | OnlineEatsBot |
| --- | --- |
| Hello OnlineEats | Hello! How may I help you? |
| I am looking to order food | Sure, What would you like to order today? |
| One chicken burger | Done. Your final amount is $3.99 |
| Thank you | Thanks a lot |

This conversation is pretty much simple and can be done without any ML model as well, even though we did use a trained model to recognize the intent and entities in it.

Now, the interesting question that will come to your mind is, "What if I want my bot to be able to change the order? What if I want my bot to be able to remove or add more quantity of the food items?" So, as discussed, add more use-cases, more complexity, more intents and their utterances, more if...else in code to handle corner-cases, but when you are building a chatbot for a business you have to scale it to generate more revenue through it. All software systems do that, and those who don't fail to survive. The bottom line is, we can't keep changing and deploying the code.

So, instead of handling all the cases as they occur and repeatedly doing it, we can take the ML route to tackle this problem, with the help of Rasa Stack, which will tell us what the bot should do next based on the user's context and the state of the conversation. Since the model learns itself based on the context of the previous conversation data, it becomes easier for the bot to keep the conversation more natural and user-friendly rather than randomly choosing from four to five fixed sentences.

Rasa recommends users with little or no data use interactive learning. We'll get to know more about **interactive learning** later in this chapter.

Before we actually start using Rasa Stack to write the core part of our bot, first we need to understand a few concepts.

# Understanding Rasa Concepts

It's really important that we understand a few specific concepts related to Rasa before actually trying to use them in code completely. In this section we'll be learning a few important and very useful concepts of Rasa NLU. Make sure you understand these concepts completely, as we will be using them in building our first in-house chatbot using Rasa's domain file format. If we do not understand what these concepts mean, then it'll be difficult to take the next step.

## Action

As the name suggests, it's a specific action that can be taken. As per Rasa documentation, it says, *"Next action to be taken in response to a dialog state."*

For example, if a user asks the horoscope for today, our bot could execute the "GetTodaysHoroscope" action. Let's see how a "GetTodaysHoroscope" action would look in form of a code.

```python
from rasa_core.actions import Action
from rasa_core.events import SlotSet

class GetTodaysHoroscope(Action):
    def name(self):
        return "get_todays_horoscope"

    def run(self, dispatcher, tracker, domain):
        # type: (Dispatcher, DialogueStateTracker, Domain) -> List[Event]

        user_horoscope_sign = tracker.get_slot('horoscope_sign')
        """Write your logic to get today's horoscope details
            for the given Horoscope sign based on some API calls
            or retrieval from the database"""

return [SlotSet("horoscope_sign", user_horoscope_sign)]
```

The **name** method returns the name of the Action that we'll refer to in the domain file as custom method name.

The **run** method does the main job for getting the action done—i.e., the core business logic resides here. As you can see, it takes three parameters: *dispatch, tracker,* and *domain.*

Let's understand these parameters one by one:

- **dispatcher:** the dispatcher is used to send messages back to our users. We can use `dipatcher.utter_message()` to achieve the same.

- **tracker:** the state tracker for the current user. We can access slot values using `tracker.get_slot(slot_name),` and to get the most recent user message we can use `tracker.latest_message.text.`

- **domain:** the bot's domain. We'll discuss in more detail about the domain later in the chapter.

---

**Note**   run method returns a list of Events instances.

---

## Slots

Slots are the ones who make the bot responsible for working like a human. Slots are like a storage space where the information given by the user can be stored or a pre-fetched information from a database or an API can also be used.

There are different slot types for different use-cases:

For example, in our use-case where we want to build a HoroscopeBot, we may want to use the slot type as **text** for the **horoscope_sign** provided by the user.

Depending on what type of slot you want to keep, Rasa provides some predefined slot types.

Other than text, Rasa has the following slot types:

- **Boolean** ⇒ Used For True/False

- **Categorical** ⇒ Used for situations where you have to pick one of some values

- **Float** ⇒ Used for continuous values

- **List** ⇒ Used for list of values

- **Featurized** ⇒ Used for internal value storage that doesn't affect the conversation

## Templates

Templates is a word you must have heard in your life at least once, while finding a template for sending an e-mail, for preparing a document, for building a portfolio website, or to follow a process.

Templates in Rasa are used for utterances. An utterance template contains a set of preset text to be sent to the user when some action is triggered. By having the same name of the action as the utterance or by an action with custom code, we can send our formatted message in templates to the user.

A simple representation of templates inside the domain file may look like the following:

```
templates:
  utter_greet:
    - "hello {name}!"    # name can be filled by a slot of same name or by
    custom code
  utter_goodbye:
    - "goodbye"
    - "take care bye"    # multiple templates allow the bot to randomly pick
    from them
  utter_default:
    - "Sorry, I didn't get that."
```

Now, that we have gone through the three concepts of actions, slots, and templates and we already know what intents and entities are as part of our learning from Chapter 3, we are now ready to dive deep into Rasa and start writing code for our first chatbot.

## Creating Domain File for the Chatbot

The first and foremost task to do while building a chatbot using Rasa stack is to create a domain file.

As per the documentation of Rasa, "The Domain defines the universe in which your bot operates. It specifies the intents, entities, slots, and actions your bot should know about. Optionally, it can also include templates for the things your bot can say."

Now, you know why we had to be prepared for this situation previously by understanding Rasa core concepts.

Let's create a DefaultDomain file with a YAML definition. Rasa uses .yml files to define the domain format.

Originally YAML supposedly meant Yet Another Markup Language, depicting its use as a markup language, but it was changed later to be understood as YAML Ain't Markup Language, a recursive acronym, to differentiate its purpose as data-oriented rather than a document markup language.

Now, let's go back to our rasa-nlu Jupyter Notebook directory and start creating the files. Note that we can write all our code in separate files using a command line and use an editor to edit it. I find Jupyter Notebook more interactive and easily accessible to browse through the files. Whatever you are comfortable with, go with that, but it is good to know most of the features that Jupyter Notebook provides.

Go to the main horoscope_bot directory and create a file, let's call it horoscope_domain.yml.

The following is the content of horoscope_domain.yml for our bot:

```
slots:
    horoscope_sign:
        type: text
    DD:
        type: text
    MM:
        type: text

    subscribe:
        type: bool

intents:
    - greeting
    - get_horoscope
    - subscription
    - dob_intent

entities:
    - horoscope_sign
    - DD
    - MM
    - subscribe
    - dob_intent
```

```
templates:
    utter_greet:
        - 'Hello! How are you doing today?'
    utter_ask_horoscope_sign:
        - 'What is your horoscope sign?'
    utter_ask_dob:
        - 'What is your DOB in DD-MM format?'
    utter_subscribe:
        - 'Do you want to subscribe for daily updates?'

actions:
    - utter_greet
    - utter_ask_horoscope_sign
    - utter_ask_dob
    - utter_subscribe
    - get_todays_horoscope
    - subscribe_user
```

As you can see, the domain file is comprised of five important parts: intents, entities, slots, templates, and actions, which we discussed earlier.

Note that for every template, there is an utterAction defined, such as utter_greet, utter_ask_horoscope_sign, and utter_ask_dob, we must have a template defined in the template section with the same name.

As you can see in our example, there are mainly five actions defined, where the first three actions are just for uttering a template text to the user, but the last two actions require us to either retrieve the data from the database or make an API call to get the horoscope for the day and return it back to the user.

In the case of subscribe_user action as well, we need to do an operation where we add the current user to the subscribe list in the database. These user-defined actions are called custom actions. To have such custom actions, we need to write what the bot is supposed to do when these actions are triggered.

In the next section we are going to learn how to write custom actions.

# Writing Custom Actions of the Chatbot

As we know, whenever an `UtterAction` is triggered, our bot will respond back with the utter text defined in the template for that Action. But what happens when some custom action is triggered? In this section we'll write Python code to create custom actions, which we can use to make API calls or pretty much any kind of thing that you can do with Python.

Let's create a new file called `actions.py` in our project directory (i.e., in our case inside `horoscope_bot` folder).

```python
from __future__ import absolute_import
from __future__ import division
from __future__ import print_function
from __future__ import unicode_literals

import requests
from rasa_core_sdk import Action
from rasa_core_sdk.events import SlotSet

class GetTodaysHoroscope(Action):

    def name(self):
        return "get_todays_horoscope"

    def run(self, dispatcher, tracker, domain):
        # type: (Dispatcher, DialogueStateTracker, Domain) -> List[Event]

        user_horoscope_sign = tracker.get_slot('horoscope_sign')
        base_url = http://horoscope-api.herokuapp.com/horoscope/{day}/{sign}
        url = base_url.format(**{'day': "today", 'sign': user_horoscope_
        sign})
        #http://horoscope-api.herokuapp.com/horoscope/today/capricorn
        res = requests.get(url)
        todays_horoscope = res.json()['horoscope']
        response = "Your today's horoscope:\n{}".format(todays_horoscope)

        dispatcher.utter_message(response)
        return [SlotSet("horoscope_sign", user_horoscope_sign)]
```

As we can see, there are two methods in our action called GetTodaysHoroscope. The first method **name** just returns the name of the action. The other method is **run** and, as discussed earlier, is the method that actually does the task by executing the business logic that we write.

In our method we are making use of an open-source API with code hosted on github [https://github.com/tapasweni-pathak/Horoscope-API]

The API url looks like this:

**http://horoscope-api.herokuapp.com/horoscope/today/capricorn**

which returns the data in JSON format:

```
{
  "date": "2018-08-29",
  "horoscope": "You will be overpowered with nostalgia and may long to get
  in touch with old pals. And as Ganesha says, chances are that you may
  take a liking to your ex-lover, while simultaneously strengthening your
  social standing. All in all, the day will be a productive one.",
  "sunsign": "capricorn"
}
```

As you can see in the **run** method, we convert the response from the API to Python JSON object and then access the 'horoscope' key from the JSON to get the actual horoscope. After getting the actual horoscope from the JSON, we formulate a response and dispatch it back to the user using the dispatcher object and its method, utter_message.

At the end we set the slot using SlotSet method. SlotSet is like saving the variables that you figured out from user's responses so that you can use them any time in your code during the flow of the conversation.

---

**Note**   Using the above API we can get today's horoscope by providing the horoscope sign. You are free to use your own API or database. You just need to replace the API call with some other source that you want to use.

---

Just like we added the GetTodaysHoroscope action in the actions.py file, we'll also add SubscribeUser action as well. We are not going to use any database to store the user subscription preferences, but when you are building a chatbot for real users, you may have to have user_ids that you can link with their subscriptions in the database.

The following is how the SubscribeUser action looks:

```python
class SubscribeUser(Action):
    def name(self):
        return "subscribe_user"

    def run(self, dispatcher, tracker, domain):
        # type: (Dispatcher, DialogueStateTracker, Domain) -> List[Event]

        subscribe = tracker.get_slot('subscribe')

        if subscribe == "True":
            response = "You're successfully subscribed"
        if subscribe == "False":
            response = "You're successfully unsubscribed"

        dispatcher.utter_message(response)
        return [SlotSet("subscribe", subscribe)]
```

Like this, we can write as many custom actions as needed.

The next step is the data. Rasa's dialog management model is trained on actual conversations that users and the chatbot do. The important point here is that those conversations have to be converted into a story format.

A story is nothing but an actual conversation between a user and a chatbot where user inputs are converted into intents and entities while responses being returned from the chatbot are treated as actions that the chatbot is supposed to trigger when it's required.

One of the examples of how a real conversation between a user and a chatbot may look as a story is given in the table below.

Scenario I

| User | HoroscopeBot |
| --- | --- |
| Hello there! | utter_greet |
| I want to know my horoscope for today | utter_ask_horoscope_sign |
| My sign is Capricorn | actions.GetTodaysHoroscope |
| Can you subscribe me for updates? | actions.SubscribeUser |

Scenario II

| User | HoroscopeBot |
|------|--------------|
| Hello there! | utter_greet |
| I want to know my horoscope for today | utter_ask_horoscope_sign |
| I don't know my sign | utter_ask_dob |
| 12-12 | actions.GetTodaysHoroscope |

We haven't yet covered the scenario in the code where the user doesn't know his horoscope sign but knows his DOB. Here, our code needs some modification to get the DATE and MONTH entities when horoscope_sign value is not found.

We could use DD-MM values to check the horoscope sign and then call the GetTodaysHoroscope method explicitly or train the model in that way.

# Data Preparation for Training the Bot

It's always important to have good quality data before doing any kind of ML. For training our chatbot we also need data; the conversation between a user and a chatbot is the data on which we need to train our models. Sometimes it becomes difficult to find a dataset freely on the web that fits our own need.

We should spend the time we need to get the data gathered. We can ask our friends and family to provide us the sample conversation text of how they would interact with a kind of bot you are building. Some people create sample example apps for the same and crowd-source the data. So, better the data, better the model, and better the chatbot responses.

When it comes to preparing the data, Rasa leaves no stone unturned and comes with a cool feature called **interactive learning**. It helps you in generating story data easily and also trains the dialog management model as we keep adding the story data. You can call it real-time ML training. So, as we keep on adding our story data, we get to know if our model is producing correct output or not. Most importantly we get to see if the model is improving or degrading when we add new stories. In most cases it will get better because we'll be kind of doing the reinforcement learning where we tell the ML model to unlearn and relearn—pretty much what human beings do.

# Creating Story Data

As we know, story data is just a way of conversation between a user and a chatbot on how it would lead to a logical end. In general, all chatbots are designed to help users with a set of predefined things; stories just represent how they are done.

We'll try to prepare some simple dialogs in the format that Rasa expects. These dialogs will be stateless—that is, they do not depend on previous dialogs. We will be using our handmade stateless stories for interactive learning.

We'll take a couple of minutes to just hand-curate a few stories that we know of, so that we get acclimatized with how story data is created.

Let's first create a file named `stories.md` in our **data** folder.

```
## story_001
* greeting
  - utter_greet
* get_horoscope
  - utter_ask_horoscope_sign
* get_horoscope{"horoscope_sign": "Capricorn"}
  - slot{"horoscope_sign": "Aries"}
  - get_todays_horoscope
  - utter_subscribe

## story_002
* greeting
  - utter_greet
* get_horoscope{"horoscope_sign": "Capricorn"}
  - slot{"horoscope_sign": "Cancer"}
  - get_todays_horoscope
  - utter_subscribe
* subscription
  - slot{"subscribe": "True"}
  - subscribe_user

## Horoscope query with horoscope_sign
* greeting
    - utter_greet
```

```
* get_horoscope
    - utter_ask_horoscope_sign
* get_horoscope{"horoscope_sign": "capricorn"}
    - slot{"horoscope_sign": "capricorn"}
    - get_todays_horoscope
    - slot{"horoscope_sign": "capricorn"}
    - utter_subscribe
* subscription{"subscribe": "True"}
    - slot{"subscribe": "True"}
    - subscribe_user
    - slot{"subscribe": true}

## Horoscope with sign provided
* greeting
    - utter_greet
* get_horoscope{"horoscope_sign": "leo"}
    - slot{"horoscope_sign": "leo"}
    - get_todays_horoscope
    - slot{"horoscope_sign": "leo"}
    - utter_subscribe
* subscription{"subscribe": "True"}
    - slot{"subscribe": "True"}
    - subscribe_user
    - slot{"subscribe": true}

## When user directly asks for subscription
* greeting
    - utter_greet
* subscription{"subscribe": "True"}
    - slot{"subscribe": "True"}
    - subscribe_user
    - slot{"subscribe": true}
```

If you stare at the stories for a couple of minutes, they will confess to you what they means; it shouldn't be difficult to make some sense of what is happening. The main difference between the first two stories is that in the first story the user doesn't mention his horoscope sign and the bot is supposed to ask the horoscope sign and then proceed with the story.

In the second story, the user himself tells the horoscope sign and then ends the story with the subscribe dialog. We have added couple of more stories covering more use-cases. Feel free to add your own stories in the same file.

So, basically stories are markdown files where we can write as many stories as needed in the markdown format shown earlier. Doing this seems a bit of a tough task by hand. So, we'll try to learn how to use Rasa's own **interactive learning** tool to generate more stories like this.

Let's get started.

# Interactive Learning

We have been talking about interactive learning in bits and pieces so far, but it's time to actually write some code and do it. Interactive learning is one of the coolest features Rasa has where it makes the ML part fun and easy. There are two parts: in the first part, we train a model by giving our initial dataset using various policies, and in the second part we test the model, correct it, and re-train it in an interactive manner.

## Training the Chatbot Agent Model

Let's create a new file called `train_initialize.py` in our main project directory. Contents of `train_initialize.py` looks like this:

```python
from __future__ import absolute_import
from __future__ import division
from __future__ import print_function
from __future__ import unicode_literals

from rasa_core import utils
from rasa_core.agent import Agent
from rasa_core.policies.keras_policy import KerasPolicy
from rasa_core.policies.memoization import MemoizationPolicy
from rasa_core.policies.sklearn_policy import SklearnPolicy

if __name__ == '__main__':
    utils.configure_colored_logging(loglevel="DEBUG")

    training_data_file = './data/stories.md'
    model_path = './models/dialogue'
```

```
agent = Agent("horoscope_domain.yml",
              policies=[MemoizationPolicy(), KerasPolicy()])

training_data = agent.load_data(training_data_file)

agent.train(
        training_data,
        augmentation_factor=50,
        epochs=500,
        batch_size=10,

        validation_split=0.2
)

agent.persist(model_path)
```

This is the code that we write in `train_initialize.py` file. Now, before we move on to the next code file, let's first try to understand important points in it.

1.  First, we import a few methods from __future__ module. Future statements in Python have special usage, they change how your Python module is parsed, and they change the way your existing method behaves.

    ```
    Curious personality ? Try the below code in your python
    interpreter
        from __future__ import braces
    ```

2.  Import `utils` method from rasa_core modules to configure logging.

3.  Import agent class from agent module to create the agent object.

4.  KerasPolicy, MemorizationPolicy will be passed as policies parameters to agent class.

5.  **configure_colored_logging:** Utility method defined in utils.py for colored logging using Python's coloredlogs package.

6.  **Agent:** A class defined by Rasa that provides an interface to make use of most important Rasa Core functionality, such as training, handling messages, loading a dialog model, getting the next action, and handling a channel.

7. **load_data:** loads training data from the given path.

8. **train:** trains the given policies/policy ensemble using data from the file provided.

9. **training_data:** object returned by **load_data** method. List of `DialogueStateTracker`. This is nothing but our training data file.

10. **augmentation_factor:** tells Rasa how many dummy stories should be created given our initial set of stories. 10x factor is a heuristic for augmentation rounds for training data generator.

11. **epochs:** 1 epoch is a complete training cycle on an entire training dataset. Total number of forward and backward passes of training data.

12. **batch_size:** tells you the amount of training sample to use in each pass. 100 examples with a batch_size of 10 will take 10 epochs to go over the entire dataset.

13. **validation_split:** percentage of data to validate the unbiased accuracy of a model.

14. **persist:** this method is used to persist the agent object in a given directory for re-use.

At this point you should be pretty much clear on what each method does and what's happening inside the code.

Before we go on to run the script, make sure you have rasa_core library installed before executing this script.

You can install rasa_core using the following command:

```
pip install rasa_core==0.11.1
```

If you are following the chatbot example in this book, then make sure you installed the aforementioned version only, as Rasa may not be backward-compatible. They are rapidly coming up with newer and more optimized methods.

---

**THE LATEST RASA_CORE**

---

You can also install the bleeding edge version of rasa_core from the github repo. You just have to execute the following set of commands, which will take the latest code from github directly before installing.

```
git clone https://github.com/RasaHQ/rasa_core.git
cd rasa_core
pip install -r requirements.txt
pip install -e .
```

---

Let's try to run this code file to train our model as per the given parameters.

`$python train_initialize.py`

You can also run this script from Jupyter Notebook itself using Jupyter's magic command, as shown here:

`!python train_initialize.py` #Use python3 if you have installed rasa for python3

It should take about 25 to 30 seconds for the model to be trained on such a small dataset as ours. I added SklearnPolicy in the list of policies along with MemorizationPolicy and KerasPolicy to train my model. Different policies have their own benefits. Read more about them to know which may work better for your use-case; for my dataset SklearnPolicy seems to be performing better than the KerasPolicy at times.

After the script is done executing you should see some successful messages like these:

```
2018-08-30 04:24:31 INFO     rasa_core.policies.keras_policy  - Done fitting
keras policy model
2018-08-30 04:24:31 INFO     rasa_core.featurizers  - Creating states and
action examples from collected trackers (by MaxHistoryTrackerFeaturizer)...
Processed trackers: 100%|███████████████████| 96/96 [00:00<00:00,
898.31it/s, # actions=75]
2018-08-30 04:24:31 INFO     rasa_core.featurizers  - Created 75 action
examples.
2018-08-30 04:24:31 INFO     rasa_core.policies.sklearn_policy  - Done
fitting sklearn policy model
```

```
2018-08-30 04:24:31 INFO    rasa_core.agent  - Model directory models/nlu
exists and contains old model files. All files will be overwritten.
2018-08-30 04:24:31 INFO    rasa_core.agent  - Persisted model to
'/Users/sumit/apress_all/Chapter IV/horoscope_bot/models/nlu'
```

You will also find a couple of folders created as per their model name. Make sure you have them in the model_path you gave in the script. Below are the folders/files I see inside my model_path folder.

```
policy_0_MemoizationPolicy
policy_1_KerasPolicy
policy_2_SklearnPolicy
domain.json
domain.yml
Policy_metadata.json
```

If you have validated that your model has successfully completed the execution and has persisted the model in your local system, then we are good to go to the next step of interactive training.

## Real-Time Training by Reinforcement

In this section we are going to write some more code to train our dialog model and retrain when it gives incorrect output.

So, when our bot does something wrong we immediately jump in and let the model know that its prediction is wrong by telling it what is right. Without having to stop, the model retrains itself, and once we are done, the interaction between the user and the bot gets captured to a file and added to our existing training data. It works more like a feedback system in every step, rather than waiting for a single reward at the end.

The next step is to create a new file called endpoints.yml with the below contents. We'll be using this file in our Python code file train_online.py. With this configuration we can expose the Rasa method as HTTP APIs.

```
action_endpoint:
  url: http://localhost:5055/webhook

#nlg:
#  url: http://localhost:5056/nlg
```

```
core_endpoint:
  url: http://localhost:5005
```

Now, let's create `train_online.py` for our online/interactive training purposes.

```python
from __future__ import absolute_import
from __future__ import division
from __future__ import print_function
from __future__ import unicode_literals

import logging

from rasa_core import utils, train
from rasa_core.training import online
from rasa_core.interpreter import NaturalLanguageInterpreter

logger = logging.getLogger(__name__)

def train_agent(interpreter):
    return train.train_dialog_model(domain_file="horoscope_domain.yml",
                                    stories_file="data/stories.md",
                                    output_path="models/dialog",
                                    nlu_model_path=interpreter,
                                    endpoints="endpoints.yml",
                                    max_history=2,
                                    kwargs={"batch_size": 50,
                                            "epochs": 200,
                                            "max_training_samples": 300
                                            })

if __name__ == '__main__':
    utils.configure_colored_logging(loglevel="DEBUG")
    nlu_model_path = "./models/nlu/default/horoscopebot"
    interpreter = NaturalLanguageInterpreter.create(nlu_model_path)
    agent = train_agent(interpreter)
    online.serve_agent(agent)
```

`max_history` is the number of states to keep track of by the model.

Before we go on to run our final script, `train_online.py`, we should know and make ourselves ready for something called rasa-nlu-sdk.

## rasa-nlu-sdk

Rasa NLU stack comes up with rasa-nlu-sdk, which is a Python SDK for the development of custom actions for Rasa Core. As for our chatbot example, we need to define a few custom actions, like hitting the API to get today's horoscope or maybe a database writing operations to add the user to the subscribe list.

The good news is they have a separate library for this, and we can install that using pip.

Let's install that using the following command:

```
pip install rasa-core-sdk==0.11.0
```

Now, we need to go to another tab of our terminal or a fresh command line and execute the following command in our project directory (the place where our `actions.py` file is):

```
python -m rasa_core_sdk.endpoint --actions actions

INFO:__main__:Starting action endpoint server...
INFO:rasa_core_sdk.executor:Registered function for 'get_todays_horoscope'.
INFO:rasa_core_sdk.executor:Registered function for 'subscribe_user'.
INFO:__main__:Action endpoint is up and running. on ('0.0.0.0', 5055)
```

This command will start an action server that will be listening to any custom action predicted by the model. As soon as any action is triggered, it will execute it and give the response as per the method.

The default port for the action server endpoint is 5055 on localhost. If you want to change it, you can add pass `--port` argument in the command line.

A quick question comes to mind: why? Why do I need a separate server for that? Why can't we use plain Python? Yes, we can use plain Python, but suppose you were to develop the required actions in any other language or you have some actions already exposed as APIs. Now, you just need to go to `endpoints.yml,` which we already created, and use that to mention from where your action server should be used and where your core_endpoint server should be. In a production system both can be different servers having altogether different urls.

Now, when we run our next script where we mentioned our endpoints.yml file, Rasa will read the file and get the configuration for our action_server, which is already up and running as per the configuration we did earlier.

```
action_endpoint:
      url: http://localhost:5055/webhook
```

Let's run the `train_online.py` in a fresh command line terminal.

```
$python3 train_online.py
```

After a successful training of the dialog model, we'll be getting a message like this:

```
2018-08-30 07:09:37 INFO     rasa_core.policies.keras_policy  - Done
fitting keras policy model
2018-08-30 07:09:37 INFO     rasa_core.agent  - Model directory models/nlu
exists and contains old model files. All files will be overwritten.
2018-08-30 07:09:37 INFO     rasa_core.agent  - Persisted model to '/Users/
sumit/apress_all/Chapter IV/horoscope_bot/models/nlu'
2018-08-30 07:09:37 INFO     rasa_core.training.online  - Rasa Core server
is up and running on http://localhost:5005
Bot loaded. Type a message and press enter (use '/stop' to exit).
127.0.0.1 - - [2018-08-30 07:09:37] "GET /domain HTTP/1.1" 200 996 0.001847
```

Now, here you can start talking to your bot that has just been born. From here it's solely in your hands how you train it. You can correct it whenever it responds something bad or unexpected.

Let's do that and see if it improves.

I enter "Hi" as the first message and the bot returns the following:

```
------------------------------------------------------------------------
```

*Chat history:*

> *bot did: action_listen*
>
> *user said: hi*
>
> *whose intent is: {'confidence': 0.8472929307505297, 'name': 'greeting'}*

*we currently have slots: DD: None, MM: None, horoscope_sign: None,*
*subscribe: None*

*------*

*The bot wants to [utter_greet] due to the intent. Is this correct?*

    *1.       Yes*
    *2.       No, intent is right but the action is wrong*
    *3.       The intent is wrong*
    *0.       Export current conversations as stories and quit*

------------------------------------------------------------------------

Now, the bot is telling me what it did based on what the user said and how he understands it. Now, it also gives us four options. We'll talk about that in a moment.

What **bot_did** here is action_listen meaning; it was just waiting for the user to enter something, which is fine.

Bot says the intent *{'confidence': 0.8472929307505297, 'name': 'greeting'}*, which is correct, so we'll press 1, meaning what the bot is understanding and trying to do it correct.

1
------------------------------------------------------------------------
Chat history:

    bot did: action_listen

    user said: hi

    whose intent is: {'confidence': 0.8472929307505297, 'name': 'greeting'}

    bot did: utter_greet

we currently have slots: DD: None, MM: None, horoscope_sign: None,
subscribe: None

------

The bot wants to [action_listen]. Is this correct?

    1.       Yes.
    2.       No, the action is wrong.
    0.       Export current conversations as stories and quit

------------------------------------------------------------------------

And there you are, our bot at least greeted the user properly. If you see the aforementioned response, you can actually check what our bot did; it keeps track of all this while we train it.

```
bot did: utter_greet
```

Now, the bot says that the next thing is to wait and listen to what the user is going to say (i.e., waiting for the user input). Is this correct? Yes, that's correct, so we press 1 again and the bot gives a prompt to the user.

I enter, "What's my horoscope for today?"

```
-------------------------------------------------------------------------
Chat history:

      bot did: action_listen

      user said: hi

            whose intent is: {'confidence': 0.8472929307505297, 'name':
            'greeting'}

      bot did: utter_greet

      bot did: action_listen

      user said: what's my horoscope for today?

      whose intent is: {'confidence': 0.8902154738608781, 'name':
      'get_horoscope'}

we currently have slots: DD: None, MM: None, horoscope_sign: None,
subscribe: None

------

The bot wants to [utter_ask_horoscope_sign] due to the intent. Is this
correct?

      1.      Yes
      2.      No, intent is right but the action is wrong
      3.      The intent is wrong
      0.      Export current conversations as stories and quit

-------------------------------------------------------------------------
```

Now, the bot very correctly identifies the intent to be "get_horoscope" intent with 89 percent accuracy, which is quite good. The bot also says that it wants to **utter_ ask_horoscope_sign,** which is correct again because the user has not mentioned any horoscope sign yet and the slot is still None, as shown.

We press 1 again.

--------------------------------------------------------------------------

```
Chat history:

      bot did: action_listen

      user said: hi

      whose intent is: {'confidence': 0.8472929307505297, 'name': 'greeting'}

      bot did: utter_greet

      bot did: action_listen

      user said: what's my horoscope for today?

      whose intent is: {'confidence': 0.8902154738608781, 'name':
      'get_horoscope'}

      bot did: utter_ask_horoscope_sign

we currently have slots: DD: None, MM: None, horoscope_sign: None,
subscribe: None

------

The bot wants to [action_listen]. Is this correct?

      1.      Yes.
      2.      No, the action is wrong.
      0.      Export current conversations as stories and quit
```

--------------------------------------------------------------------------

Now, the bot asks if it's time to wait for the user input. Yes, the user needs to provide the horoscope sign.

We press 1 again, and when prompted, we entered "Capricorn" as the input.

------------------------------------------------------------------------

Chat history:

    bot did: action_listen

    user said: hi

    whose intent is: {'confidence': 0.8472929307505297, 'name': 'greeting'}

    bot did: utter_greet

    bot did: action_listen

    user said: what's my horoscope for today?

    whose intent is: {'confidence': 0.8902154738608781, 'name':
    'get_horoscope'}

    bot did: utter_ask_horoscope_sign

    bot did: action_listen

    user said: Capricorn

    whose intent is: {'confidence': 0.8456705103362621, 'name':
    'get_horoscope'}

    with horoscope_sign: capricorn

we currently have slots: DD: None, MM: None, horoscope_sign: capricorn,
subscribe: None

The bot wants to [get_todays_horoscope] due to the intent. Is this correct?

    1.      Yes
    2.      No, intent is right but the action is wrong
    3.      The intent is wrong
    0.      Export current conversations as stories and quit

------------------------------------------------------------------------

Now, as we can see, the horoscope_sign slot is automagically set above to "**Capricorn**."

The next step is to teach the bot to call **get_todays_horoscope** and to call the **get_todays_horoscope** action. By this time our slot is already set for the *horoscope_sign* variable that we defined in horoscope_domain.yml, so if this action is called again, the chatbot should return the actual horoscope for the day. Let's try.

I entered "Capricorn."

The bot hits the action server's endpoint and brings the result back to the user as we defined in our custom action.

```
Your today's horoscope:
```

The journey from defeat to success is driven by optimism. You will be very optimistic today—about your work, future, and everything that can lead you to success, says Ganesha. You will also be very careful while dealing with day-to-day work, and will capitalize on every opportunity that can get you a step closer to your goals. Determination and good luck is all you need to realize your dreams; you will have both today.

This seems fair, as I am missing my deadline to complete this chapter, and right now it's 6:00 AM in the morning and I have not slept yet. Doing every bit so that your money is worth spending on this book.

Okay, let's get back to see what our bot is trying to do next.

```
------
The bot wants to [action_listen]. Is this correct?

    1.      Yes.
    2.      No, the action is wrong.
    0.      Export current conversations as stories and quit
```

Maybe we don't want our bot to listen now after it has uttered the horoscope for today. We want our bot to ask for the user to subscribe to the updates as per our conversation script and also as per the stories we created.

So, I would press 2, and it says

```
------
What is the next action for the bot?

        0                          action_listen      1.00
        1                          action_restart      0.00
        2                 action_default_fallback      0.00
```

| | | |
|---|---|---|
| 3 | utter_greet | 0.00 |
| 4 | utter_ask_horoscope_sign | 0.00 |
| 5 | utter_ask_dob | 0.00 |
| 6 | utter_subscribe | 0.00 |
| 7 | get_todays_horoscope | 0.00 |
| 8 | subscribe_user | 0.00 |

Since we want our user to subscribe, we should press 6 so that the bot asks the user if he/she wants to subscribe for daily updates.

The bot replies, "Do you want to subscribe for daily updates?"

Now the bot says:

```
-----------------------------------------------------------------------
The bot wants to [get_todays_horoscope]. Is this correct?

    1.       Yes.
    2.       No, the action is wrong.
    0.       Export current conversations as stories and quit
```

The action here is not correct, so we press 2 and train the bot to listen to the user's action here.

```
-----------------------------------------------------------------------
what is the next action for the bot?
```

| | | |
|---|---|---|
| 0 | action_listen | 0.21 |
| 1 | action_restart | 0.01 |
| 2 | action_default_fallback | 0.01 |
| 3 | utter_greet | 0.21 |
| 4 | utter_ask_horoscope_sign | 0.51 |
| 5 | utter_ask_dob | 0.01 |
| 6 | utter_subscribe | 0.02 |
| 7 | get_todays_horoscope | 0.78 |
| 8 | subscribe_user | 0.22 |

```
-----------------------------------------------------------------------
```

We press 0 when the bot is waiting to know the correct next step. The bot will now wait for the user input in our interactive learning process.

The user says here, "Please subscribe me," and our bot successfully with 80 percent confidence recognizes this to be a subscription intent and also, based on our training data in data.json, understands pretty easily that the user is asking to subscribe and not unsubscribe. In other words, it sets the slot of subscribe to True, as you can see here:

```
------------------------------------------------------------------

    user said: Please subscribe me

    whose intent is: {'confidence': 0.795172441763619, 'name':
    'subscription'}

    with subscribe: True

we currently have slots: DD: None, MM: None, horoscope_sign: capricorn,
subscribe: True

------------------------------------------------------------------
```

Now, that our bot has understood the intent and also parsed the entities in it, it's time to reply back to the user saying, "He is successfully subscribed," and bingo—we get a message from bot:

```
You're successfully subscribed
```

There you go! You can successfully build your own in-house chatbot all by yourselves. As a part of the exercise, I would recommend you add all use-cases we discussed for HoroscopeBot and see if it works. Try to add more uses-cases and more functionality when everything we have done so far works well.

You can add more utterance messages here for the bot to say, "Goodbye, have a good day," after the conversation is completed. I strongly believe you should be in a position to do that. Make sure you do that and let us know how it went for you.

Now, the final part is to give all of this learning back to the user so that we don't have to teach the same stories again and the bot tries to learn from the existing stories and more to come.

# Exporting Conversations As Stories

Now the next step in the interactive learning part is to press 0 and export our current conversations as stories and quit.

We press 0 for that and the bot prompts something like this:

```
File to export to (if file exists, this will append the stories) [stories.md]:
```

Just enter our **stories.md** filename, if you have kept any other name, then make sure you give the correct filename.

And Rasa does the hard job for us and generates a stories.md file for us automagically again like this:

```
## Generated Story 3797421409943253925
* greeting
    - utter_greet
* I want to know my horoscope
    - utter_ask_horoscope_sign
* get_horoscope

## Generated Story 7304374603374920907
* greeting
    - utter_greet
* what is my todays horoscope?
    - utter_ask_horoscope_sign
* Cancer

## Generated Story -6877464862083507836
* greeting
    - utter_greet
* get_horoscope
    - utter_ask_horoscope_sign
* get_horoscope{"horoscope_sign": "capricorn"}
    - slot{"horoscope_sign": "capricorn"}
    - get_todays_horoscope
    - slot{"horoscope_sign": "capricorn"}
    - utter_subscribe
* subscription{"subscribe": "True"}
    - slot{"subscribe": "True"}
    - subscribe_user
    - slot{"subscribe": true}
```

You can either change the source of the stories file while training the model with the aforementioned file or you can copy and paste the newly generated stories into our original stories.md file. For now, I am going to copy and paste these stories in our original stories.md file. Make sure to run your models again before testing or doing interactive learning again.

# Testing the Bot

Testing the bot is a part of our interactive learning process. We keep checking all the possible scenarios initially thought for the bot and train it accordingly. I tested Horoscope Bot for some other scenarios and trained it accordingly. The following is one of them that is a bit different than what we did earlier in this chapter.

## Test Case 1

Let's run the first test:

> **User:** Hello there!
>
> **HoroscopeBot:** Hello! What can I do for you?
>
> **User:** What's the horoscope for Capricorn today?
>
> **HoroscopeBot:** Your today's horoscope:

The journey from defeat to success is driven by optimism. You will be very optimistic today—about your work, future, and everything that can lead you to success, says Ganesha. You will also be very careful while dealing with day-to-day work, and will capitalize on every opportunity that can get you a step closer to your goals. Determination and good luck is all you need to realize your dreams; you will have both today.

> **HoroscopeBot:** Do you want to subscribe for daily updates?
>
> **User:** Please subscribe me.
>
> **HoroscopeBot:** You're successfully subscribed.

As you can see in this conversation between the user and the chatbot, we tested if the bot handles the scenario where the user himself provides the horoscope_sign while asking for the horoscope for the day itself. The bot does well in this case and ends up asking for a subscription and, based on the user response, takes appropriate action.

You should do a sanity testing of the bot's conversation to determine if normal flow is working or not.

I also tested the story we mentioned in our stories.md file when a user directly asked for a subscription and it worked as well.

## Test Case 2

Now the second test:

> **User:** Hi
>
> **HoroscopeBot:** Hello! What can I do for you?
>
> **User:** Subscribe me please for daily updates.
>
> **HoroscopeBot:** You're successfully subscribed.

I will be adding a couple of more new stories as well so that the bot works flawlessly. But as of now we have a fully working bot. In the second version of the code on github you will also find the bot to be correcting the spelling mistakes for horoscope sign, retrieving horoscope sign based on user's DOB, saying a goodbye message, etc. I strongly recommend you check the code on how it is done and provide your feedback. But before that, give a thought to how it'll be done and where the changes will go. We have knowingly not mentioned the code for the other use-cases in this chapter, so that it doesn't become fussy while you are concentrating on learning the tricks of the trade.

You can download the latest Python code and Jupyter Notebooks from our github repo and try to install the correct packages to run it. You will find more use-cases handled in the code as discussed in this chapter.

## Summary

In this chapter, we learned about Rasa-NLU and why Rasa-NLU is better than any other open-source tool available on the market. We learned how to configure pipelines by using tensorflow, sklearn, and keras in our pipeline configurations.

We learned to create everything from scratch on our local system without being dependent on any services requiring you to use their APIs, like Dialogflow, wit.ai, etc.

We also learned how to create stories and how to train an NLU model and a dialog model and use them both using Rasa Core to build a bot by training using the coolest feature, interactive learning. We also got a fair idea of how to create training data easily and annotate that easily with help of the open-source tools like rasa-nlu-trainer. I hope this chapter was more interactive for you than any other chapter. If you are not having a feeling of achievement, then brace yourself for the next chapter, where we'll be actually taking it live to our audiences and showing the world what bots are capable of. We'll be learning to integrate the chatbot from this chapter to various platforms like Facebook and Slack using our own web servers.

Keep training your bot until in the next chapter we take it live.

See you in the next chapter.

# CHAPTER 5

# Deploying Your Chatbot

In this chapter we'll learn how to deploy our chatbots on the web. There are various ways and channels through which one can deploy or expose their chatbot web application to the outside world. For an example, we can expose our HoroscopeBot with NLU and dialog model on Facebook and Slack as they provide you a user interface already. You may also want to have your own web app that exactly runs on your own server. We will also explore how to deploy a chatbot on our own servers using our own user interface by the end of this chapter.

## First Steps

The first step is to create a copy of your existing chatbot you built in Chapter 4 and make a new copy so that you have a backup with you. Since, we will be doing some changes by adding some new code, let's keep both the projects separate.

So, I created a new folder called "**Chapter V**" and pasted my horoscope_bot folder in there. So, now all my model files, datasets, and code files are copied, which I can directly use for deployment.

## Rasa's Credential Management

Rasa provides a way to manage all your credentials at one place. You may have one single model, but you may want it to be deployed on various other platforms like Facebook, Slack, Telegram, etc. All of these third-party platforms need some credentials to be used while connecting. These credentials are stored in a YAML file called credentials.yml.

Let's create a file named credentials.yml file in our project directory horoscope_bot folder and add our Facebook credentials there. If you don't know how to get that then just create the file for now, and in next section of this chapter you can find the steps to get Facebook credentials.

© Sumit Raj 2019
S. Raj, *Building Chatbots with Python*, https://doi.org/10.1007/978-1-4842-4096-0_5

Contents of `credentials.yml` will look like this:

```
facebook:
  verify: "horoscope-bot"
  secret: "bfe5a34a8903e745e32asd18"
  page-access-token: "HPaCAbJJ1JmQ7qDedQKdjEAAbO4iJKr7H9nx4rEBAAuFk4Q3g
  PQcNTOwtD"
```

These credentials are dummy credentials; the length of the token or secret and characters type may differ for your Facebook app.

If you are working on a big project where you are integrating your chatbot on various platforms and you want to make the project more maintainable, then it's best to make use of `credentials.yml`. I highly recommend you maintain a `credentials.yml` if you are a business and trying to build a bot that works on various platforms like Facebook, Slack, Twitter, Telegram, or your own website in the same way. Managing keys and secrets becomes easier in this case.

A good way to manage application-level secret keys is to store the keys as environment variables and write the code to read the values of secret keys or any other sensitive information from the operating system's environment itself. Remember, it's never a good idea to keep any kind of keys inside your code.

You can also create a dot(.) env file on your server and read keys from this file, which is not tracked anywhere in your code repository.

For the sake of simplicity, we are going to use the access keys and secret keys in our standalone scripts for deployment. We are going to make it simple to understand so that you are first able to build the bot, then you can try to scale it, and most importantly you can think about security-level issues.

In case you need to deploy your bot on multiple platforms and want to use credentials.yml to maintain different credentials, then you can use it by passing an extra argument. For an example to use the above credentials file named `credentials.yml` while running rasa core you can use the below command.

```
python -m rasa_core.run -d models/dialogue -u models/nlu/current
--port 5002 --credentials credentials.yml
```

It is good to know for bigger enterprise-level chatbots development, but as discussed, we'll be using the credentials directly in our script in our upcoming examples.

# Deploying the Chatbot on Facebook

In this section we are first going to deploy our chatbot using Heroku in cloud. Heroku is a platform-as-a-service (PaaS) that enables developers to build, run, and operate applications entirely in the cloud. The benefit of Heroku is that we can easily get our app running on https without much pain. We don't need to go and buy SSL certificates while we are learning and testing our chatbots. The reason why https is required is because some platforms like Facebook do not allow developers to use non-https urls as callback URLs.

We'll be following a set of steps one-by-one to successfully deploy our chatbot as a web service in cloud. Once we have done that successfully, it will be way easier to integrate it with different platforms like Slack, Telegram, etc. So, let's start.

## Creating an App on Heroku

Let's get started:

Sign up on Heroku, create an app, and name it something-actions, as this is going to be our actions server app. Have a look at the screenshot in Figure 5-1, where you can give a unique name for your actions server, which should be available on Heroku. Once that name seems available, you can click on the Create app button to create the actions server app.

Feel free to name it anything you want if your name is not available, but always try to give meaningful names.

*Figure 5-1.* *Creating the action server app on Heroku with the name horoscopebot1212-actions*

# Setting Up Heroku on Your Local System

Install Heroku CLI on your local operating system. Refer to this link: `https://devcenter.heroku.com/articles/heroku-cli`.

If you are on macOS, use the following command:

```
brew install heroku/brew/heroku
```

# Creating and Setting Up an App at Facebook

To be able to deploy our chatbot on Facebook, first we need to have credentials of the Facebook app. In order to get the Facebook credentials, we need to set up a Facebook app and a page, like we did in one of our Chapter 3.

1. Go to `https://developers.facebook.com/` and create an app if you don't have one already. We created one for our OnlineEatsBot; now we'll create one for HoroscopeBot. Enter the details and click on Create App ID. Check Figure 5-2 to see how to enter the display name of your bot and your contact email.

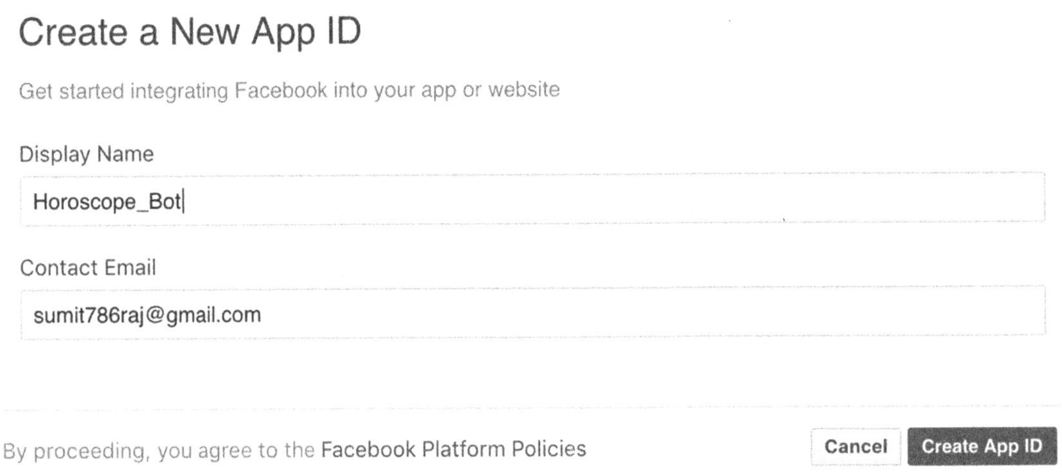

## Create a New App ID

Get started integrating Facebook into your app or website

Display Name

Horoscope_Bot|

Contact Email

sumit786raj@gmail.com

By proceeding, you agree to the Facebook Platform Policies

Cancel    Create App ID

***Figure 5-2.*** *Creating app on Facebook for developers*

2. Once your app is created, go to Basic under Settings, and click on the Show button under App Secret. This is your `fb_secret`. Refer Figure 5-3 to see where exactly you will get your `fb_secret` key.

Figure 5-3. *Getting App Secret from Facebook's app*

3. Go to the dashboard for the app and scroll down to "Add a Product." Click Add Product and then add Messenger (click on SetUp). Check Figure 5-4.

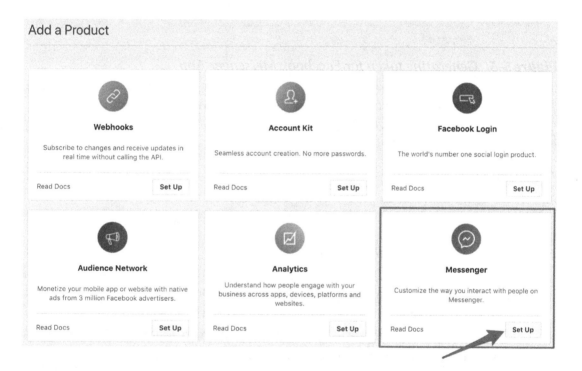

Figure 5-4. *Adding Messenger as product to Facebook app*

4. Under settings for Messenger, when you scroll down to the Token Generation section you will get a link to create a new page for your app. If you don't have a page already, then create it or choose a page from the "Select a page" dropdown. The "Page Access Token" is your fb_access_token here. Refer Figure 5-5.

You can go to the following link to create a brand new page for your bot project:

```
https://www.facebook.com/pages/creation/
```

**Figure 5-5.** *Generating token for Facebook Messenger App*

5.   Right after the Token Generation section, under Webhooks, click on "Setup Webhooks." Refer Figure 5-6.

**Figure 5-6.** *Setting up Facebook Webhooks*

6.   Next, choose a verify token, which we'll need to use later. The verify token can be any random string. This will be your `fb_verify`. Check Figure 5-7 to understand where to add the verification token in facebook app. Now, leave the callback URL section blank as it is. Don't close the browser; just leave it—we'll come back here again.

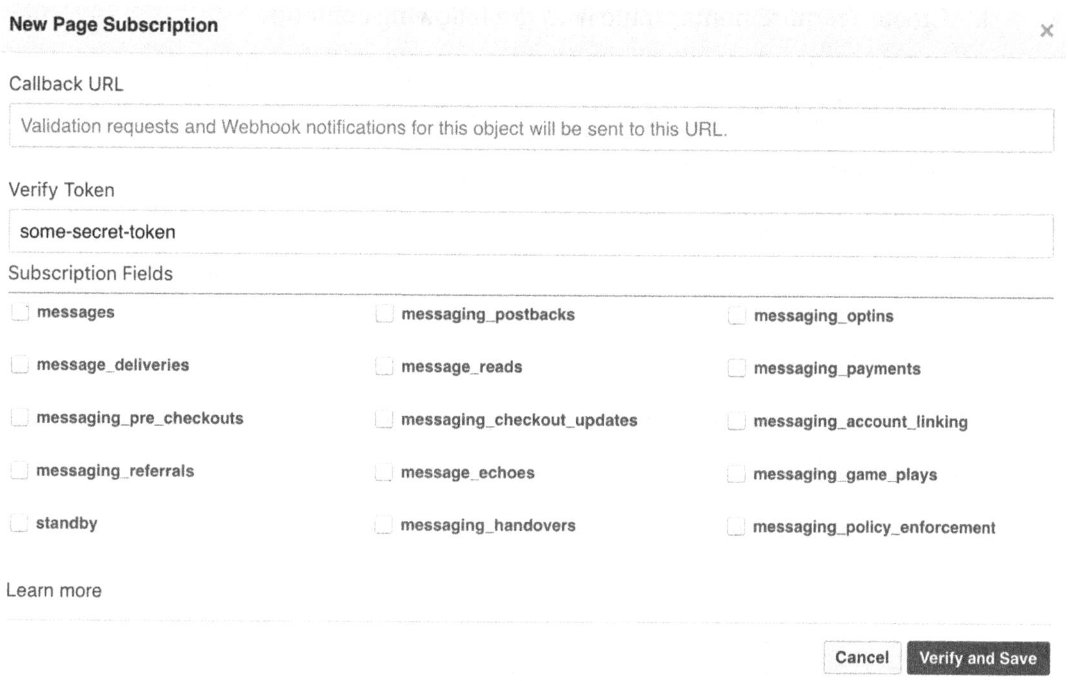

**New Page Subscription**                                                                    ✕

Callback URL

| Validation requests and Webhook notifications for this object will be sent to this URL. |

Verify Token

| some-secret-token |

Subscription Fields

| ☐ messages | ☐ messaging_postbacks | ☐ messaging_optins |
| ☐ message_deliveries | ☐ message_reads | ☐ messaging_payments |
| ☐ messaging_pre_checkouts | ☐ messaging_checkout_updates | ☐ messaging_account_linking |
| ☐ messaging_referrals | ☐ message_echoes | ☐ messaging_game_plays |
| ☐ standby | ☐ messaging_handovers | ☐ messaging_policy_enforcement |

Learn more

Cancel    **Verify and Save**

*Figure 5-7.* *Adding verify token to Facebook webhook setup*

7. Keep fb_verify, fb_secret and fb_access_token handy to connect your bot to Facebook.

# Creating and Deploying Rasa Actions Server App on Heroku

In this step we are going to use our actions Heroku app for our Rasa action's server. We need to have two different applications, as we cannot run two web applications in a single Heroku app. Go to your command line and execute the following set of commands from your project directory as directed.

1. Create a new folder called actions_app and get into the directory:

```
mkdir actions_app
cd actions_app
```

2. Copy your actions.py from main project directory to actions_app directory.

161

3.  Create a requirements.txt file with the following contents.
    `requirements.txt` will tell the Heroku app to install the packages
    with their versions.

    ```
    rasa-core-sdk==0.11.0
    requests==2.18.4
    ```

4.  Create a file named Procfile with the following contents. Procfile is
    the file for which Heroku understands what to do in order to crank
    up the applications.

    ```
    web: python -m rasa_core_sdk.endpoint --actions actions
    --port $PORT
    ```

    a)  Run the below set of commands:

    ```
    $ heroku login
    $ git init
    $ heroku git:remote -a <your-heroku-app-name>
    $ heroku buildpacks:set heroku/python
    $ heroku config:set PORT=5055
    $ git add .
    $ git commit -am "deploy my bot"
    $ git push heroku master
    ```

After the last command, Heroku will install all our packages needed as per the
requirements.txt file. If your app is successfully deployed, you should be getting logs
similar to the following:

```
remote:
remote: -----> Discovering process types
remote:          Procfile declares types -> web
remote:
remote: -----> Compressing...
remote:          Done: 48.3M
remote: -----> Launching...
remote:          Released v4
remote:          https://horoscopebot1212-actions.herokuapp.com/ deployed to
                 Heroku
```

```
remote:
remote: Verifying deploy... done.
To https://git.heroku.com/horoscopebot1212-actions.git
 * [new branch]      master -> master
```

At this point, we will just verify whether our app is responding to public requests. In order to do that let's hit the app url appended by "webhook."

App url in my case is `https://horoscopebot1212-actions.herokuapp.com/` so I'll go and check if my action's server is responding.

I go to this url `https://horoscopebot1212-actions.herokuapp.com/webhook`, and as expected, it comes back saying method not allowed, like in Figure 5-8, which is totally fine and means that app is responding correctly as per the user request.

# Method Not Allowed

The method is not allowed for the requested URL.

*Figure 5-8.*  *Verifying action server endpoint*

## Creating Rasa Chatbot API App

In this step we will follow some steps and commands similar to what we just did, but this is a new app we'll create that will be our main app for dialog management. So, let's do it. First come back to the main project directory (i.e., in horoscope_bot) and create a file name (**Procfile**) and add the following contents to it:

```
web: python -m spacy download en && python facebook.py
```

# Creating a Standalone Script for Facebook Messenger Chatbot

Create a file name facebook.py in the same project directory. The contents of the Python file should be as given here:

```
from rasa_core.channels.facebook import FacebookInput
from rasa_core.agent import Agent
from rasa_core.interpreter import RasaNLUInterpreter
import os
from rasa_core.utils import EndpointConfig

# load your trained agent
interpreter = RasaNLUInterpreter("models/nlu/default/horoscopebot/")
MODEL_PATH = "models/dialog"
action_endpoint = EndpointConfig(url="https://horoscopebot1212-actions.
herokuapp.com/webhook")

agent = Agent.load(MODEL_PATH, interpreter=interpreter)

input_channel = FacebookInput(
        fb_verify="YOUR_FB_VERIFY_TOKEN",
        # you need tell facebook this token, to confirm your URL
        fb_secret="YOUR_FB_SECRET",  # your app secret
        fb_access_token="YOUR_FB_ACCESS_TOKEN"
        # token for the page you subscribed to
)
# set serve_forever=False if you want to keep the server running
s = agent.handle_channels([input_channel], int(os.environ.get('PORT',
5004)), serve_forever=True)
```

Make sure to replace the fb_verify, fb_secret, and fb_access_token variable values in this code with what we kept in Step 3.

Create a new requirements.txt file and add all the packages and their versions needed for this project. My requirements.txt looks like the following; for your project the requirements may differ, but these requirements should be fine if you are following the same bot example in this chapter.

```
rasa-core==0.11.1
rasa-core-sdk==0.11.0
rasa-nlu==0.13.2
gunicorn==19.9.0
requests==2.18.4
spacy==2.0.11
sklearn-crfsuite==0.3.6
```

to install our packages in the server.

Now let's create a new app again in Heroku like we did earlier. Go to your Heroku dashboard and create a new app as shown in Figure 5-9.

**Figure 5-9.** *Creating dialog management app in Heroku*

Once you have created the app, you can now go to your project root directory and run the following set of commands from the command line in your project folder:

```
$ git init
$ heroku git:remote -a <your-heroku-app-name>
$ heroku buildpacks:set heroku/python
$ heroku config:set PORT=5004
$ git add .
$ git commit -am "deploy my bot"
$ git push heroku master
```

If you get a runtime error after deployment, it may look like below this

ValueError: You may be trying to read with Python 3 a joblib pickle generated with Python 2. This feature is not supported by joblib.

This will mainly happen if you are using Python 2.x version. Heroku, by default, uses Python 3.x version. So, in case you want to use Python 2.x, you need to perform the steps below to resolve the above error. Change Python 3.6 to Python-2.7.15. to do this.

Create a file runtime.txt under root app directory of your project. Open the runtime. txt and add the following line python-2.7.15 and then save it. Heroku will use the aforementioned Python version only to build your project.

Once the successful deployment is done, you will see a url Heroku gives saying the app deployed to <url>.

```
remote: Compressing source files... done.
remote: Building source:
remote:
remote: -----> Python app detected
remote: -----> Installing requirements with pip
remote:
remote: -----> Discovering process types
remote:          Procfile declares types -> web
remote:
remote: -----> Compressing...
remote:          Done: 254M
remote: -----> Launching...
remote:          Released v17
remote:          https://horoscopebot1212.herokuapp.com/ deployed to Heroku
remote:
remote: Verifying deploy... done.
To https://git.heroku.com/horoscopebot1212.git
    cd3eb1b..c0e081d  master -> master
```

This deployment is going to take a little time, so be patient as much as you can—you are about to see magic. If you didn't get any error messages, then you have successfully deployed your chatbot to Heroku on cloud to make it work with Facebook Messenger. Let's verify if it works.

# Verifying the Deployment of Our Dialog Management App on Heroku

To verify if our dialog management app is successfully deployed on Heroku, we'll be doing the following steps.

1. Take the url given by Heroku and append this endpoint to it: `/webhooks/facebook/webhook?hub.verify_token=YOUR_FB_VERIFY_TOKEN&hub.challenge=successfully_verified`. Make sure to use the correct verify token that you used for webhooks settings in Facebook. The complete url for me looks like the below: `https://horoscopebot1212.herokuapp.com/webhooks/facebook/webhook?hub.verify_token=my-secret-verify-token&hub.challenge=success`.

2. Go to the browser and paste the entire url, and it should return your hub.challenge value back if your hub.verify_token is correct. Your complete url will look like the following: `https://horoscopebot1212.herokuapp.com/webhooks/facebook/webhook?hub.verify_token=YOUR_FB_VERIFY_TOKEN&hub.challenge=successsfully_verified`. If you get the message `successsfully_verified in the browser` then your app is successfully deployed and working.

# Integrating Webhook With Facebook

Now let's go back to our Facebook app configuration. We'll go to the point where we left off in Step 3 and add our callback URL. Make sure to check the **messages** in Subscription Fields. Check Figure 5-10 for reference.

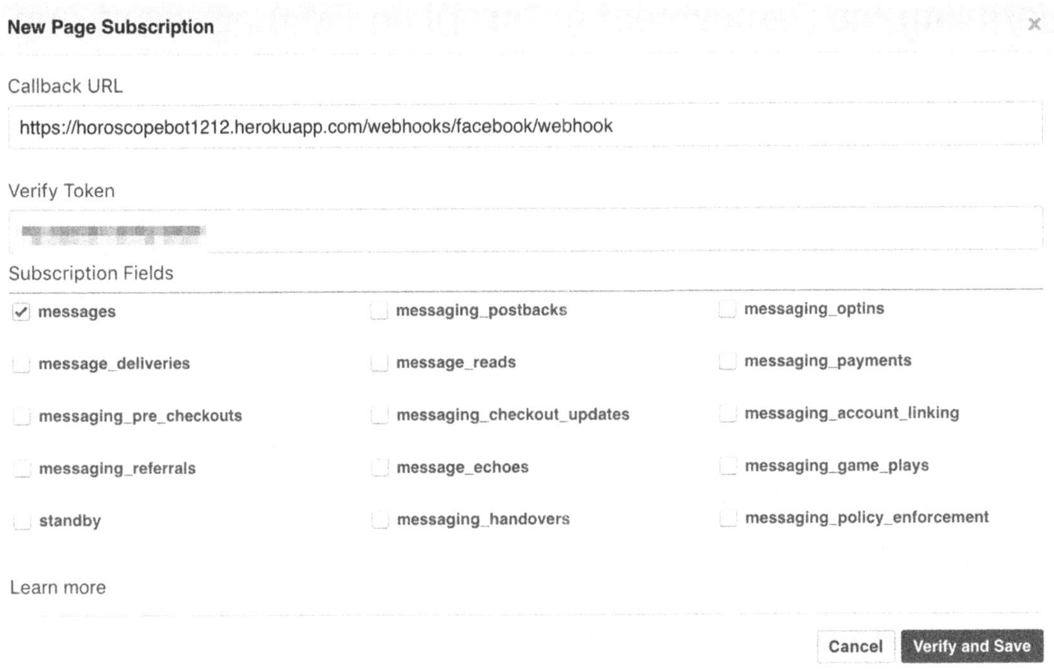

**New Page Subscription**                                                     ×

Callback URL

https://horoscopebot1212.herokuapp.com/webhooks/facebook/webhook

Verify Token

Subscription Fields

| ☑ messages | ☐ messaging_postbacks | ☐ messaging_optins |
| ☐ message_deliveries | ☐ message_reads | ☐ messaging_payments |
| ☐ messaging_pre_checkouts | ☐ messaging_checkout_updates | ☐ messaging_account_linking |
| ☐ messaging_referrals | ☐ message_echoes | ☐ messaging_game_plays |
| ☐ standby | ☐ messaging_handovers | ☐ messaging_policy_enforcement |

Learn more

Cancel    **Verify and Save**

***Figure 5-10.*** *Facebook Messenger webhooks configuration*

Click on "Verify and Save." Facebook will match the verify token using the above url, meaning the server, or say our app will only respond to requests that have the correct verify token. Once the verify token matches, the webhook subscription will get activated for our app.

Next, select a page to which you can subscribe your webhook to the page events, under the Webhooks section on the page. Click on subscribe (see Figure 5-11).

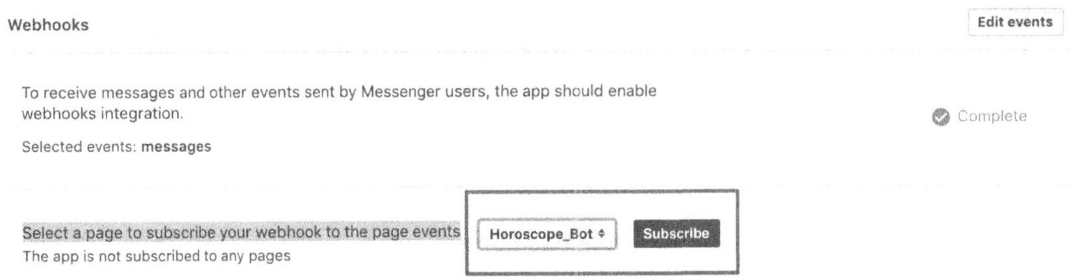

**Webhooks**                                                            Edit events

To receive messages and other events sent by Messenger users, the app should enable
webhooks integration.                                                   ✓ Complete
Selected events: **messages**

Select a page to subscribe your webhook to the page events | Horoscope_Bot ⇕ | **Subscribe**
The app is not subscribed to any pages

***Figure 5-11.*** *Subscribe webhook to Facebook page events*

All done! Time to test our Horoscope Bot on Facebook.

# Post-Deployment Verification: Facebook Chatbot

In normal software development scenarios, people build software, test it, and then deploy and do PDV (post-deployment verification). We'll also be doing something similar, and we'll do a PDV for our chatbot after our successful deployment on Facebook Messenger. This is important because, as you learned, the chatbot has a part where it needs to connect to the actions server to respond to some intent requests of the user. PDV is like a sanity testing to see that the health of the app is good overall. If you are building a bot that uses 10 to 15 different vendors' APIs, then it's a must to check all scenarios where your bot hits the action server and uses the API to return data back to the user.

So, go to your messenger app or Facebook in your computer browser and search for your bot to start talking.

Figures 5-12.1 through 5-12.3 show what my Horoscope Bot does and tells me.

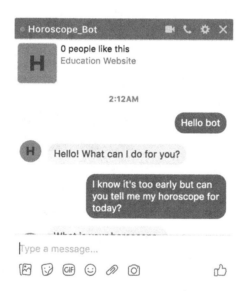

***Figure 5-12.1.*** *Horoscope_Bot Facebook*

***Figure 5-12.2.*** *Horoscope_Bot Facebook*

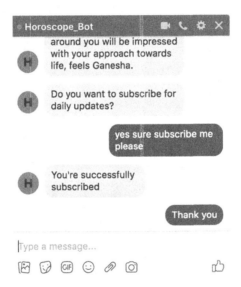

***Figure 5-12.3.*** *Horoscope_Bot Facebook*

Voila! Our first in-house-built chatbot app is deployed on the web and can be accessed via the Facebook Messenger platform. So, go ahead and share it with your family, friends, colleagues, and the entire world.

# Deploying the Chatbot on Slack

In this section we'll be deploying our chatbot to Slack. Slack is a team collaboration tool widely popular among developers and corporations. If you are not a social media person, then you might need Slack's help to talk to your chatbot using an interface. So, let's dive into building our first in-house Slack chatbot.

In order to deploy our Horoscope Chatbot to slack, we'll be writing a standalone script just like we did in the case of Facebook.

# Creating a Standalone Script for Slack Chatbot

Create a new file called slack.py in your project's directory. Contents of the file slack.py will look like the following:

```
from rasa_core.channels.slack import SlackInput
from rasa_core.agent import Agent
from rasa_core.interpreter import RasaNLUInterpreter
import os
from rasa_core.utils import EndpointConfig

# load your trained agent
interpreter = RasaNLUInterpreter("models/nlu/default/horoscopebot/")
MODEL_PATH = "models/dialogue"
action_endpoint = EndpointConfig(url="https://horoscopebot1212-actions.
herokuapp.com/webhook")

agent = Agent.load(MODEL_PATH, interpreter=interpreter, action_
endpoint=action_endpoint)

input_channel = SlackInput(
        slack_token="YOUR_SLACK_TOKEN",
        # this is the `bot_user_o_auth_access_token`
        slack_channel="YOUR_SLACK_CHANNEL"
        # the name of your channel to which the bot posts (optional)
    )
# set serve_forever=False if you want to keep the server running
s = agent.handle_channels([input_channel],  int(os.environ.get('PORT',
5004)), serve_forever=True)
```

The primary difference between `facebook.py` and `slack.py` is the `input_channel` object that we create. Rasa provides various in-built channels like Facebook, Slack, Mattermost, Telegram, Twilio, RocketChat, and Microsoft Bot Framework, which we can use directly to deploy the same bot on various channels easily.

As you can see, we need to add a `slack_token` and `slack_channel` to be added into our script. As we had to create a Facebook application on Facebook's developer platform, similarly we'll have to create an app on Slack as well.

Let's do this step by step:

1. Got to this url `https://api.slack.com/slack-apps` and click on the button "Create App." Refer Figure 5-13.

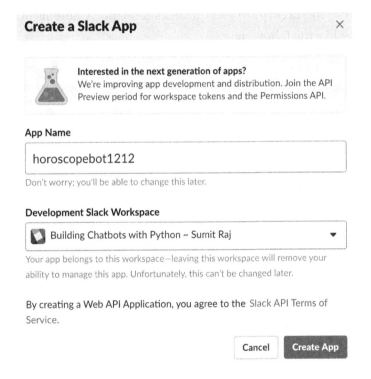

***Figure 5-13.*** *Creating an application in Slack*

2. The next step is to create a Bot User. To create a bot user, click on **Bots** under "Add features and functionality." In the new page you will get an option to "Add a Bot User.". Check Figure 5-14 to see how to add details and add a bot user.

# Bot User

You can bundle a bot user with your app to interact with users in a more conversational manner. Learn more about how bot users work.

**Display name**

Horoscope Bot using Python

Names must be shorter than 80 characters, and can't use punctuation (other than apostrophes and periods).

**Default username**

horoscopebot1212

If this username isn't available on any workspace that tries to install it, we will slightly change it to make it work. Usernames must be all lowercase. They cannot be longer than 21 characters and can only contain letters, numbers, periods, hyphens, and underscores.

**Always Show My Bot as Online**
When this is off, Slack automatically displays whether your bot is online based on usage of the RTM API.

 On

**Add Bot User**

***Figure 5-14.*** *Giving a name to your bot on Slack*

3.  Fill in the details as per the chatbot you are building. Display name can be anything that you like; default username has to be unique; you can let it be as it is. Toggling the last option to always show my bot as online is to always show the bot to be available as a user. This is what chatbots are meant for—humans can't be available 24/7, but chatbots can, so we turn on this feature. Make sure you click on save changes.

4.  Go back to the "Basic Information" tab. Click "Install your app to your workspace." The app will ask to confirm the identity. Please authorize it like you do for any other app. Check Figure 5-15 which shows how the authorization would look like.

173

On Building Chatbots with Python ~ Sumit Raj,
horoscopebot1212 would like to:

Confirm your identity on Building Chatbots with
Python ~ Sumit Raj

⚠  Add a bot user with the username                    ▶
    @horoscopebot1212

| Cancel | **Authorize** |

*Figure 5-15.  Authorizing your Slack app*

You will find the Bots and Permissions tab under "Add features and functionality" with a green checkmark, which means our bot and app are well-integrated. This is a sign that we are doing good so far.

5.    Go to your OAuth & Permissions section, and copy **Bot User OAuth Access Token.**

6.    Paste the copied token into our Python script `slack.py`. Give a channel name as you like. If you want your bot to post to a channel, then you can give a channel name. I have given @slackbot. If you do not set the `slack_channel` keyword argument, messages will be delivered back to the user who sent them.

# Editing your Procfile

In this step we won't be creating any new Procfile, as we are working with the same codebase. We'll be changing our existing Procfile to the following to make it work for our slack bot. So, we just change the name of the script file from `facebook.py` to `slack.py` so that Heroku uses the given file to start up the application.

```
web: python -m spacy download en && python slack.py
```

# Final Deployment of Slack Bot to Heroku

To finally deploy our new Slack bot to Heroku, we'll be running a similar set of Heroku commands from command line to deploy our application.

```
$ git init
$ heroku git:remote -a <your-heroku-app-name>
$ git add .
$ git commit -am "deploy my bot"
$ git push heroku master
```

# Subscribe to Slack Events

Now, click on the "**Event Subscriptions**" tab and activate the events subscriptions functionality by toggling the button on the screen. Enter the Heroku app's webhook url for Slack.

If your app was deployed on Heroku properly with the modified Procfile, your webhook url for Slack will be `app_url + /webhooks/slack/webhook`, which looks like the following:

```
https://horoscopebot1212.herokuapp.com/webhooks/slack/webhook
```

You will see a verified tick mark after Slack sends a HTTP POST request to the above URL with a challenge parameter, and our endpoint must respond with the challenge value. This is similar to what we discussed while building Facebook chatbot's secret token. Check Figure 5-16 to understand more.

# Event Subscriptions

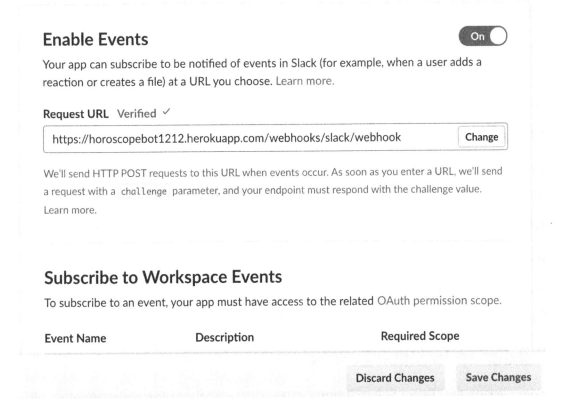

**Figure 5-16.** *Activate event subscriptions for your bot*

## Subscribe to Bot Events

In this step we'll simply scroll down the events subscriptions page and go to the "Subscribe to Bot Events" section, and click on "Add Bot User Event." Take reference of Figure 5-17 to understand where to navigate.

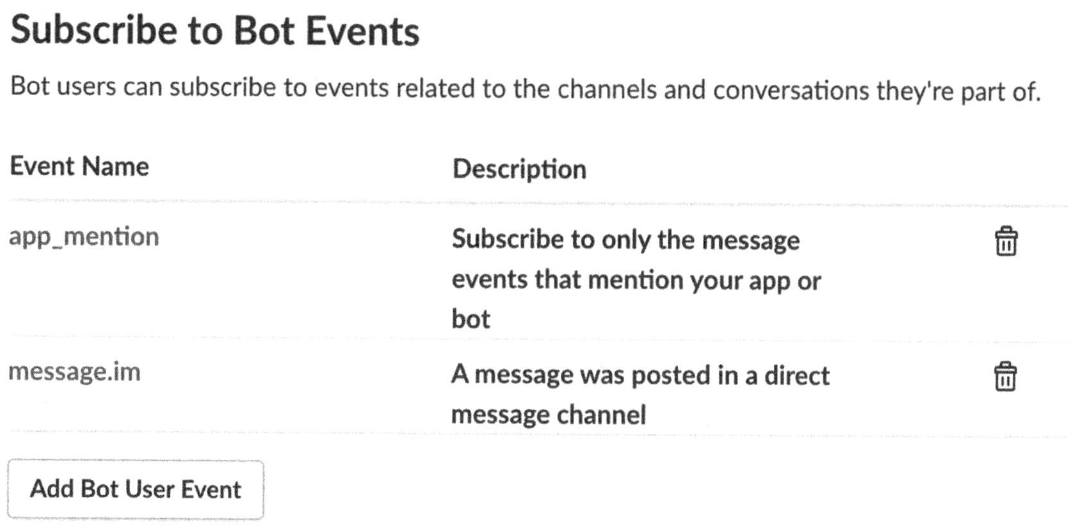

## Subscribe to Bot Events

Bot users can subscribe to events related to the channels and conversations they're part of.

| Event Name | Description | |
|---|---|---|
| app_mention | Subscribe to only the message events that mention your app or bot | 🗑 |
| message.im | A message was posted in a direct message channel | 🗑 |

Add Bot User Event

***Figure 5-17.*** *Subscribe to bot events*

Subscribe to bot events is nothing but declaring the events for which the bot has to reply. We'll only be demonstrating two scenarios here: first, when somebody mentions the bot's name (i.e., **app_mention**), and second, when somebody directly sends the bot the message (i.e., **message.im**).

Now, click on save changes, and you are done. It's time to test our Slack chatbot like we did in the previous section for Facebook.

## Post-Deployment Verification: Slack Bot

Let's go to our workspace we used to create the app, and under Apps on the left side you will find your bot. Try to talk to it and see if it does well. My bot does pretty well to give me my horoscope for today, which is good to read. If you have not been able to come till this point then check Figure 5-18 to see how my Slack bot responds.

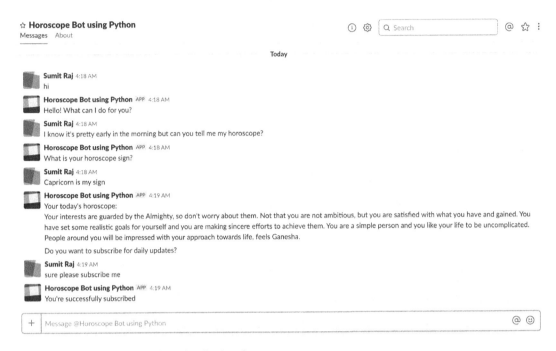

***Figure 5-18.***  *Testing the Slack chatbot*

So, folks we are done with our Slack Bot. In the next section, we'll be deploying our bot to our own UI. Building your own UI may require some front-end skills, but do not worry—we have plans for that.

# Deploying the Chatbot on Your Own

Well the caption sounds cool, doesn't it? So far, we have been deploying our chatbot on the web using Facebook or Slack, or we could have used Telegram, etc., but now it's time to deploy everything on our own—our own servers, our own data, and our own configured model using our own user interface. If you are an organization or a budding entrepreneur, you may have your bot idea on Facebook, Twitter, or Slack, but you would always want it to be working on your own websites as well so that your brand value increases more and more as the user base increases.

In this section we are going to use all our hard work so far to finally build a chatbot, which is fully functional and independent from any third-party API calls or tools like Dialogflow, wit.ai, Watson, etc. You will have all the control in the world to tweak your chatbot the way you want and, most importantly, scale it the way you want to millions of people easily.

So, let's get started.

The first step is to ensure that two of our apps that we have deployed so far in the previous sections are up and running. You already know how to do a basic sanity check. You always need your dialog manager app and actions app to be running to use your chatbot model on any platform.

Now, in the same project directory where we have been creating facebook.py and slack.py, we'll create a new file called myown_chatbot.py. The scripts created previously, like facebook.py and slack.py, are standalone scripts that we created so that we can just tell Heroku in a command which script to run to crank up the application. Now, we are creating our own script that will expose the request/response between a user and the chatbot via REST APIs.

Deploying your own chatbot has two parts. In the first part, we'll be writing a script to create a custom channel and deploy it as REST APIs. In the second part, we need our own UI, because so far, we have been using Facebook's and Slack's chat screens for the conversations.

# Writing a Script for Your Own Chatbot Channel

This script is similar to what we have learned and written so far, but it needs us to override some of the existing methods of rasa_core so that we can define our own rule for API authentication. I have done the basic string check for token verification in the following code. This is not suggested for production-level systems, so make sure to write that part with care if you are building a chatbot for larger systems.

Create a new file named myown_chatbot.py and add the following contents to it:

```
import os

from rasa_core.channels.rasa_chat import RasaChatInput
from rasa_core.agent import Agent
from rasa_core.interpreter import RasaNLUInterpreter
from rasa_core.utils import EndpointConfig

# load your trained agent
interpreter = RasaNLUInterpreter("models/nlu/default/horoscopebot/")
MODEL_PATH = "models/dialogue"
action_endpoint = EndpointConfig(url="https://horoscopebot1212-actions.
herokuapp.com/webhook")
```

```python
agent = Agent.load(MODEL_PATH, interpreter=interpreter, action_endpoint=
action_endpoint)

class MyNewInput(RasaChatInput):
    def _check_token(self, token):
        if token == 'mysecret':
            return {'username': 1234}
        else:
            print("Failed to check token: {}.".format(token))
            return None

input_channel = MyNewInput(url='https://horoscopebot1212.herokuapp.com')
# set serve_forever=False if you want to keep the server running
s = agent.handle_channels([input_channel],  int(os.environ.get('PORT',
5004)), serve_forever=True)
```

A couple of points to be noted here:

- _check_token method in rasa_core basically looks like the following,
  which makes an API call to get the user object. This primarily does
  the job of user-level authentication/authentication. In the earlier
  overridden method, we have kept it simple to make it work and
  understand its usage.

```python
def _check_token(self, token):
        url = "{}/users/me".format(self.base_url)
        headers = {"Authorization": token}
        logger.debug("Requesting user information from auth server {}."
                    "".format(url))
        result = requests.get(url,
                                headers=headers,
                                timeout=DEFAULT_REQUEST_TIMEOUT)

        if result.status_code == 200:
            return result.json()
        else:
            logger.info("Failed to check token: {}. "
                        "Content: {}".format(token, request.data))
            return None
```

- Using Rasa's own _check_token method may require you to write one API or web service that accepts the request and returns the response in the specified way.

- Make sure to change the action's server endpoint to your own url.

- Remember the mysecret string in the code will be used to make the API calls later.

## Writing the Procfile and Deploying to the Web

By this time you must be pretty familiar with creating Procfiles for Heroku deployment. We'll again use our existing Procfile and do the modifications there to deploy our API-based chatbot to the web. Feel free to create a new Procfile after creating backups of existing ones.

The following is what my Procfile content looks like:

```
web: python -m spacy download en && python myown_chatbot.py
```

Once you are done, just execute the next set of commands that we already learned while deploying our Facebook Messenger and Slack Bot.

```
$ git init
$ heroku git:remote -a <your-heroku-app-name>
$ git add .
$ git commit -am "deploy my bot"
$ git push heroku master
```

After the last command you will get some logs from Heroku related to deployment version, changes made to the app, etc.

## Verifying Your Chatbot APIs

After getting a successful message for deployment, let's test if our chatbot APIs are working or not. In order to quickly do the sanity testing, hit the following url:

```
<your-basic-app-url>+/webhooks/rasa/
```

**Example**:

```
https://horoscopebot1212.herokuapp.com/webhooks/rasa/
```

Opening this url in the browser should give you a response like the following. If it gives you a status of "ok," then you are good to go—just relax, sit back, and debug.

{"status":"ok"}

Sometimes, just this verification may not be enough, so let's test it for real by trying to check if the chatbot is working to identify the intents and giving responses based on that.

I will be using the POSTMAN tool (POSTMAN is a very nice GUI-based tool to do API testing). You can use any tool you are comfortable with. We are just going to test one of the intents our chatbot is supposed to understand and respond to. I tested the greetings intent and it worked like a charm. The bot came back with an expected response as shown in Figure 5-19.

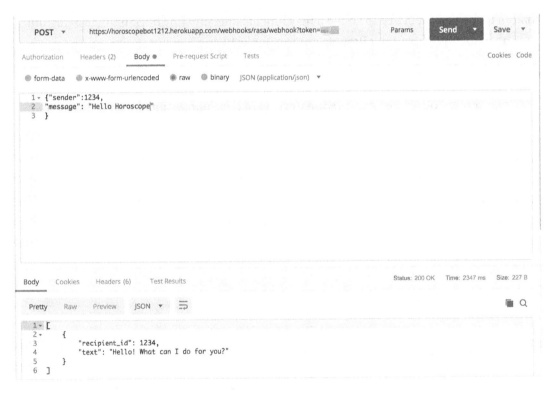

***Figure 5-19.*** *Testing chatbot API in POSTMAN*

# Creating the Chatbot UI

As we discussed earlier, as a part of the second step, we need to have our own UI to give a user-friendly place for conversation between the chatbot and the user. If you are a front-end developer or you have a front-end developer on the team, you can easily give the chatbot APIs we built to this point, and the front-end team should be easily able to integrate this with their chatbot UI. They can make use of regular HTTP calls to consume these APIs. Websockets are a better way of doing chatbots, but that is not under the scope of this book to explain.

If you are not familiar with front-end technologies like HTML/CSS/Javascript, then I do recommend *Pro HTML5 with CSS, JavaScript, and Multimedia* (Apress, 2017).

For our reader's—or, I should say, learner's—convenience we have created a basic UI required for a chatbot and user conversation. You will find the entire working code on github or Apress's website. I am just going to tell you the configuration needed to make it work for your bot.

Once you download the code for this chapter you will find the folder inside the main folder called my_own_chatbot. Go to this folder and go to assets -> js -> script.js file.

Change the following line of javascript code to your own endpoint url. If your app name was different then below url will be different in your case. Use your own url with the token in the javascript code as shown in the url below.

```
var baseUrl = "https://horoscopebot1212.herokuapp.com/webhooks/rasa/
webhook?token=YOUR-SECRET";
```

Save the file and open the index.html file in the browser and you could easily see a chatbot UI ready. But making API calls from simple HTML being served locally raises a CORS issue. So, to avoid this situation we are going to change our existing myown_chatbot.py a bit to serve the HTML from our Heroku app itself.

Change your myown_chatbot.py to the below and then we'll discuss the changes made.

```
import os

from rasa_core.channels.rasa_chat import RasaChatInput
from rasa_core.channels.channel import CollectingOutputChannel, UserMessage
from rasa_core.agent import Agent
from rasa_core.interpreter import RasaNLUInterpreter
from rasa_core.utils import EndpointConfig
from rasa_core import utils
```

```python
from flask import render_template, Blueprint, jsonify, request

# load your trained agent
interpreter = RasaNLUInterpreter("models/nlu/default/horoscopebot/")
MODEL_PATH = "models/dialogue"
action_endpoint = EndpointConfig(url="https://horoscopebot1212-actions.
herokuapp.com/webhook")

agent = Agent.load(MODEL_PATH, interpreter=interpreter, action_endpoint=
action_endpoint)

class MyNewInput(RasaChatInput):
    @classmethod
    def name(cls):
        return "rasa"

    def _check_token(self, token):
        if token == 'secret':
            return {'username': 1234}
        else:
            print("Failed to check token: {}.".format(token))
            return None

    def blueprint(self, on_new_message):
        templates_folder = os.path.join(os.path.dirname(os.path.abspath(__
        file__)), 'myown_chatbot')

        custom_webhook = Blueprint('custom_webhook', __name__, template_
        folder = templates_folder)

        @custom_webhook.route("/", methods=['GET'])
        def health():
            return jsonify({"status": "ok"})
        @custom_webhook.route("/chat", methods=['GET'])
        def chat():
            return render_template('index.html')

        @custom_webhook.route("/webhook", methods=['POST'])
        def receive():
```

```
    sender_id = self._extract_sender(request)
    text = self._extract_message(request)
    should_use_stream = utils.bool_arg("stream", default=False)

    if should_use_stream:
        return Response(
                self.stream_response(on_new_message, text,
                sender_id),
                content_type='text/event-stream')
    else:
        collector = CollectingOutputChannel()
        on_new_message(UserMessage(text, collector, sender_id))
        return jsonify(collector.messages)

    return custom_webhook

input_channel = MyNewInput(url='https://horoscopebot1212.herokuapp.com')
# set serve_forever=False if you want to keep the server running
s = agent.handle_channels([input_channel],  int(os.environ.get('PORT',
5004)), serve_forever=True)
```

Here are the changes that we made:

- Override the existing name and blueprint method in our class, which lets us create our own endpoint and also gives us the liberty to define how it should behave.

- We created a new endpoint/chat and served the index.html file, which is nothing but the UI for chatbot. So, this will be the home link for our chatbot.

- We had to import some necessary classes and methods, like utils, CollectingOutputChannel, and UserMessage as needed to make things work.

Save the file and deploy the changes again to our Heroku app using the following commands:

```
$ git add .
$ git commit -am "deploy my bot"
$ git push heroku master
```

Once deployed successfully—Voila! We have our bot ready to be shared with the entire world, which works using two Heroku apps: one for dialog management and one for actions.

Open the following url in the browser where we should see our custom chatbot UI:

```
https://horoscopebot1212.herokuapp.com/webhooks/rasa/chat
```

Figures 5-20.1 and 5-20.2 show how my own chatbot looks during the conversation.

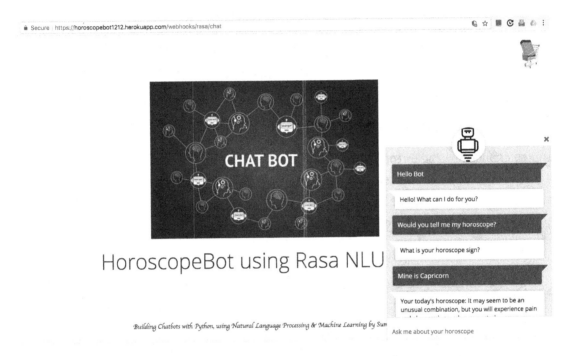

***Figure 5-20.1.*** *Your own custom chatbot on your own website*

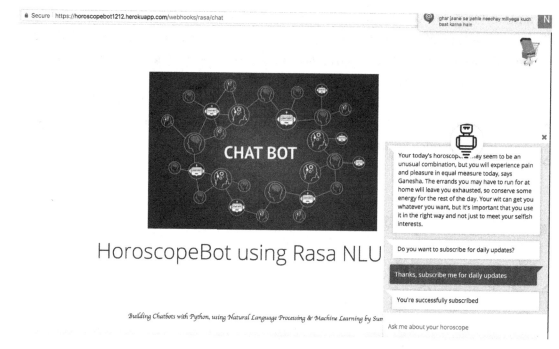

**Figure 5-20.2.** *Your own custom chatbot on your own website*

Using Heroku's custom domain name features, one can easily point the same app to their own website's name, like `www.example.com`. Do that when you feel your chatbot is good enough to be opened to the entire world for profit or non-profit purposes.

So, that's all folks! That's how chatbots are built with Python using Natural Language Processing and machine learning. I hope this chapter along with the previous chapters was helpful to you and you could learn the practical approach toward learning and building chatbots.

# Summary

In this chapter, we learned how to deploy our own app to our own servers using Heroku. We learned how to integrate our chatbot with Facebook using Facebook's developer platform. We also learned to create a custom chatbot for a Slack app and tested it as well. Finally, as promised at the end of chapter-III, removing all dependencies from any social media platform platform, we created our own UI and deployed it on Heroku and tested it. We saw it working like a charm—it worked while training it. As we have a basic model up and working, now you can handle cases where chatbot doesn't work well. Determine if it's an issue related to data or training, actions server, or custom code handling. Once you find the root case, fix that, deploy again, and check to see if chatbot improves. We build big software by starting small.

I am looking forward to hearing from you and curious to know what chatbot you built after going through this book. I will be happy to help you anytime if you are stuck on any concepts, code execution, or deployment.

Thanks and Cheers.

# Index

© Sumit Raj 2019
S. Raj, *Building Chatbots with Python*, https://doi.org/10.1007/978-1-4842-4096-0

## G

## H

## I, J, K, L, M

## N, O

## P

## Q

## R

Printed in the United States
By Bookmasters